PENGU

SPEAI

A. K. Ramanujan was born in South India and has deg[illegible] English and in Linguistics. He has held teaching appointments at the Universities of Baroda (India), Wisconsin, Berkeley, Michigan, Indiana and Chicago. He has contributed articles in linguistics, folklore and Indian literature to many journals and books; his poetry and translations (from Kannada, Tamil, and Malayalam) have been widely published in India, the United States, and Great Britain. His publications include *Proverbs* (in Kannada, 1955), *The Striders* (Poetry Book Society Recommendation, 1966), *The Interior Landscape* (translations from Classical Tamil, 1970), *Hokkulalli Hūvilla* (Kannada poems, 1969), and *Relations* (poems, 1971).

SPEAKING OF ŚIVA

★

TRANSLATED WITH AN

INTRODUCTION BY

A. K. RAMANUJAN

PENGUIN BOOKS

Penguin Books Ltd, Harmondsworth, Middlesex, England
Viking Penguin Inc., 40 West 23rd Street, New York, New York 10010, U.S.A.
Penguin Books Australia Ltd, Ringwood, Victoria, Australia
Penguin Books Canada Ltd, 2801 John Street, Markham, Ontario, Canada L3R 1B4
Penguin Books (N.Z.) Ltd, 182–190 Wairau Road, Auckland 10, New Zealand

—

First published 1973
Reprinted 1979, 1985, 1987

—

—

Printed and bound in Great Britain by
Cox & Wyman Ltd, Reading
Set in Monotype Bembo

This is one of the volumes sponsored by the Asian Literature Program of the Asia Society.

Versions of these translations appeared in: *The East-West Review*, Spring and Summer 1966, Volume II, Number 3; *TriQuarterly*, Number 11, Winter 1968; *Vedanta & the West*, November/December 1970, Number 206; and *Transpacific*, Number 7, Volume II, Number 3, Spring 1971.

This book has been accepted in the Indian Translations Series of the United Nations Educational, Scientific and Cultural Organization (Unesco).

for my father
Attippat Āsūri Krishnaswāmi
(1892–1953)

Contents

Translator's Note

Speaking of Śiva is a book of *vacanas*. A *vacana* is a religious lyric in Kannada free verse; vacana means literally 'saying, thing said'.

Kannada is a Dravidian language, spoken today in the south Indian state of Mysore by nearly 20 million people. Of the four major Dravidian languages, Kannada is second only to Tamil in antiquity of literary tradition. There is evidence for at least fifteen centuries of literary work in Kannada. Yet in all the length and variety of this literature, there is no body of lyrics more strikingly original and impassioned than the vacanas of the medieval *Vīraśaiva*[1] saints. They all speak of Śiva and speak to Śiva: hence the title.

The most intense and significant period of vacana poetry was a span of two centuries between the tenth and the twelfth. Four saints of the period are represented here: Dāsimayya, Basavaṇṇa, Allama, and Mahādēviyakka, without doubt the greatest poets of the vacana tradition. Though vacanas continue to be written to this day and later writers have occasionally composed striking ones, not one of the later 300 or more *vacanakāras* comes anywhere close to these four saint-poets in range, poetry, or passion.[2]

1. '*Vīraśaiva*' means 'militant or heroic śaivism or faith in Śiva'. The Vīraśaivas are also commonly known as liṅgāyatas: 'those who wear the *liṅga*, the symbol of Śiva'. Orthodox liṅgāyatas wear the liṅga, stone emblem of Śiva, in a silver casket round their necks symbolizing His personal and near presence. Śiva, the 'auspicious one', is elsewhere one of the Hindu trinity of gods: Brahma the creator, Viṣṇu the preserver, Śiva the destroyer. In the vacanas, Śiva is the supreme god.

2. Many thousand vacanas are attributed to each major saint. The legends, given to excesses, speak of millions. Over 300 vacana-writers

In these Vīraśaiva saint-poets, experience spoke in a mother tongue. Pan-Indian Sanskrit, the second language of cultured Indians for centuries, gave way to colloquial Kannada. The strictness of traditional metres, the formality of literary genres, divisions of prose and verse, gave way to the innovations and spontaneity of free verse, a poetry that was not recognizably in verse. The poets were not bards or pundits in a court but men and women speaking to men and women. They were of every class, caste and trade; some were outcastes, some illiterate.

Vacanas are literature, but not merely literary. They are a literature in spite of itself, scorning artifice, ornament, learning, privilege: a religious literature, literary because religious; great voices of a sweeping movement of protest and reform in Hindu society; witnesses to conflict and ecstasy in gifted mystical men. Vacanas are our wisdom literature. They have been called the Kannada Upaniṣads. Some hear the tone and voice of Old Testament prophets or the Chuang-Tzu here. Vacanas are also our psalms and hymns. Analogues may be multiplied. The vacanas may be seen as still another version of the Perennial Philosophy. But that is to forget particulars.

Faced with such an embarrassment of riches, no clear principle would do for the choice of poems for translation. So, giving in to the vacana spirit, I have let the vacanas choose me, letting them speak to my biases; translating whatever struck me over the past two decades. A translation has to be true to the translator no less than to the originals. He cannot jump off his own shadow. Translation is choice,

---

are known to date. Many more are being discovered. Several thousand vacanas are in print and on palmleaf. Scholars at the Karnatak University, Dharwar, and elsewhere, are engaged in the task of collecting, collating and editing the manuscripts.

interpretation, an assertion of taste, a betrayal of what answers to one's needs, one's envies. I can only hope that my needs are not entirely eccentric or irrelevant to the needs of others in the two traditions, the one I translate from and the one I translate into. I have tried to choose (a) good poems, (b) poetry representative of the poet, (c) poems thematically typical of the vacana tradition, and (d) a few unique in idea, image, or form.

In the act of translating, 'the Spirit killeth and the Letter giveth Life'. Any direct attack on the 'spirit of the work' is foredoomed to fuzziness. Only the literal text, the word made flesh, can take us to the word behind the words. I have tried therefore to attend closely to the language of the originals, their design, detail by detail; not to match the Kannada with the English, but to *map* the medieval Kannada onto the soundlook of modern English; in rhythm and punctuation, in phrase-breaks, paragraphs and lineation to suggest the inner form of the originals as I see them. Medieval Kannada manuscripts use no punctuation, no paragraph-, word-, or phrase-divisions, though modern editions print the vacanas with all the modern conventions. The few liberties I have taken are towards a close structural mimicry, a re-enactment in English, the transposition of a structure in one texture onto another. Valéry said of a translation of St John of the Cross: 'This is really to *translate*, which is to reconstitute as nearly as possible the *effect* of a certain cause'. The relevant formal features of the vacanas are discussed in the Introduction.

There are three parts to this book: an introduction, the poems, appendixes and notes. There are short biographical notes on each of the four saint-poets represented. The book ends with two appendixes, one on Vīraśaiva religious philosophy, and one on the contemporary Lingayat community by anthropologist William McCormack; and notes on a few textual points and allusions.

The editions I have used are acknowledged at the end of each section-note. The poems follow the Kannada editions in numbering and arrangement.

NOTE ON TRANSLITERATION

The transliteration system used for Kannada names and words in this book is very close to the accepted Sanskrit transliteration system. The only difference is in marking length for the mid-vowels e ē o ō, whereas Sanskrit has only ē ō. Words of Sanskrit origin are given in their Kannada forms: e.g., Kāmalatā in Sanskrit would become Kāmalate in Kannada. I have transliterated the *anusvāra* by the appropriate nasal which one hears in pronunciation: e.g. for *liṁga*, I write *liṅga*.

VOWELS

	FRONT		CENTRAL		BACK	
	short	*long*	*short*	*long*	*short*	*long*
HIGH	i	ī			u	ū
MID	e	ē			o	ō
LOW			a	ā		
Diphthongs:		ai				
		au				

CONSONANTS

	velar[1]	*palatal*	*retroflex*	*alveolar*	*dental*	*labial*
stops[2]	k kh	c ch	ṭ ṭh		t th	p ph
	g gh	j jh	ḍ ḍh		d dh	b bh
nasals	ṅ	ñ	ṇ	n		m
fricatives	h	ś	ṣ	s		
liquids			ḷ	l r		
semivowels		y				v

1. Velar, palatal etc. indicate positions of articulation.
2. Stops, nasals etc. indicate manner of articulation.

The above charts indicate rather roughly the phonetic values of the letters. A few striking features of Kannada pronunciation may be pointed out for the use of English readers interested in trying to pronounce the Kannada words the Kannada way.

1. Kannada long vowels are simple long vowels, unlike their English counterparts, which are (usually) diphthongs as in *beet, boot, boat.*

2. Among other things, Kannada has three kinds of consonants unfamiliar to English speakers: the dentals (t th d dh), the retroflexes (ṭ ṭh ḍ ḍh ṇ ṣ ḷ), the aspirated stops (kh gh ch jh th dh ṭh ḍh ph bh).

The dentals are pronounced with the tongue stopping the breath at the teeth, somewhat like French or Italian dentals, in words like *tu, du, Dante.*

The retroflexes are made by curling back the tongue towards the roof of the mouth, somewhat as in some American English pronunciations of *party, morning, girl.*

The Kannada sounds represented by ph, th, ch, kh, etc. are aspirated (but more strongly) like English word-initial stops as in *pin, kin, tin.* In Kannada, even the voiced stops bh, dh, gh, etc. are aspirated, unlike any English voiced consonant. The sounds represented by p t ṭ c k are unaspirated everywhere, sounded somewhat like the English consonants in *spin, stain, skin.*

3. There are no alveolar stops in Kannada corresponding to English t, d; but Kannada s, l, n are produced by the tongue at the alveolar position as in English.

4. There are long (or double) consonants in the middle of Kannada words. English has them only across words: *hot tin, seven nights, sick cow* etc. They are indicated in the texts by double letters as in Kannada, Basavaṇṇa.

5. The Kannada r is flapped or trilled somewhat as in the British pronunciation of *ring, berry.*

Acknowledgements

IN translating medieval Kannada to modern English, many hands and minds have helped. My thanks are due to The Asia Society, New York, and personally to Mrs Bonnie Crown, Director of the Asian Literature Program, for support, publishers, advice, deadlines streaked with kindness; William McCormack for an anthropological essay on Lingayat Culture written specially for this volume (pp. 175–187); M. Cidananda Murti, who read critically each translation, checked it against the texts and his accurate learning; M. G. Krishnamurti, Girish Karnad and C. Kambar, who read and discussed with me the early drafts and increased my understanding of the poetry of the originals; Leonard Nathan, poet and translator, for his suggestions regarding the English detail; my colleagues, Edward Dimock, Milton Singer, J. A. B. van Buitenen, Norman Zide and Ron Inden, for discussions on bhakti; the Staff of the Department of South Asian Languages and Civilization for making the illegible legible, in more senses than the obvious; my wife for her scepticism and her faith; her perceptions have chastened and enriched page after page.

Acknowledgements have to stop somewhere. 'What do I have that I have not received?'

Chicago, 1969 A. K. RAMANUJAN

Introduction

THE TEMPLE AND THE BODY

The rich
will make temples for Śiva.
What shall I,
a poor man,
do?

My legs are pillars,
the body the shrine,
the head a cupola
of gold.

Listen, O lord of the meeting rivers,
things standing shall fall,
but the moving ever shall stay.

BASAVAṆṆA 820

BASAVAṆṆA was the leader of the medieval religious movement, Vīraśaivism, of which the Kannada vacanas are the most important texts. If one were to choose a single poem to represent the whole extraordinary body of religious lyrics called the vacanas, one cannot do better than choose the above poem of Basavaṇṇa's. It dramatizes several of the themes and oppositions characteristic of the protest or 'protestant' movement called Vīraśaivism.

For instance: Indian temples are traditionally built in the image of the human body. The ritual for building a temple begins with digging in the earth, and planting a pot of seed. The temple is said to rise from the implanted seed, like a human. The different parts of a temple are named after body parts. The two sides are called the hands or wings, the *hasta*; a pillar is called a foot, *pāda*. The top of the temple is the head, the *śikhara*. The shrine, the innermost and the darkest sanctum of the temple, is a *garbhagṛha*, the womb-house. The temple thus carries out in brick and stone the primordial blueprint of the human body.[1]

But in history the human metaphor fades. The model, the meaning, is submerged. The temple becomes a static standing thing that has forgotten its moving originals. Basavaṇṇa's poem calls for a return to the original of all temples, preferring the body to the embodiment.

The poems as well as the saints' legends suggest a cycle of transformations – temple into body into temple, or a circle of identities – a temple is a body is a temple. The legend of saint Ghaṇṭākarṇa is a striking example: when the saint realized that Śiva was the supreme god, he gave himself as an offering to Śiva. His body became the threshold of a Śiva temple, his limbs the frame of the door, his head the temple bell.

The poem draws a distinction between *making* and *being*. The rich can only *make*[2] temples. They may not *be* or become temples by what they do. Further what is made is a mortal artifact, but what one *is* is immortal (lines 11–12).

This opposition, the standing *v.* the moving, *sthāvara v. jaṅgama*, is at the heart of Vīraśaivism. The Sanskrit word *sthāvara*, containing the same Indo-European root as in English words like 'stand', 'state', 'estate', 'stature', 'static', 'status', carries connotations of these related words. Jaṅgama contains a cognate of English *go*. Sthāvara is that which stands, a piece of property, a thing inanimate. Jaṅgama

1. Some interpreters extend the symbolism further: if a temple has three doors, they represent the three states of consciousness (sleep, waking, and dream) through any of which you may reach the Lord within; if it has five doors, they represent the five senses etc.

2. A distinction often found in Indo-European languages between making and doing is suggested by lines 2 and 5. Kannada has only one word for both: 'māḍu'.

is moving, moveable, anything given to going and coming. Especially in Vīraśaiva religion a Jaṅgama is a religious man who has renounced world and home, moving from village to village, representing god to the devoted, a god incarnate. Sthāvara could mean any static symbol or idol of god, a temple, or a liṅga worshipped in a temple. Thus the two words carry a contrast between two opposed conceptions of god and of worship. Basavaṇṇa in the above poem prefers the original to the symbol, the body that remembers to the temple that forgets, the poor though living moving jaṅgama to the rich petrified temple, the sthāvara, standing out there.

The poem opens by relating the temple to the rich. Medieval South Indian temples looked remarkably like palaces with battlements; they were richly endowed and patronized by the wealthy and the powerful, without whom the massive structures housing the bejewelled gods and sculptured pillars would not have been possible. The Vīraśaiva movement was a social upheaval by and for the poor, the low-caste and the outcaste against the rich and the privileged; it was a rising of the unlettered against the literate pundit, flesh and blood against stone.

The poem enacts this conflict. Lines 1–5 speak of 'making temples'. 'They' are opposed to 'I', the poor man, who can neither make nor do anything. In lines 6–9 the poet recovers from the despair with an assertion of identities between body and temple; legs are pillars, the body a shrine, the head a cupola, a defiant cupola of *gold*. From 'making' the poem has moved to 'being'. Lines 10–12 sum up the contrasts, asserting a universal: What's *made* will crumble, what's standing will fall; but what *is*, the living moving *jaṅgama*, is immortal.

The first sentence of the poem has a clear tense,[3] placing

3. In one textual variant, the tense is the future tense; in others, the past.

the making of temples in time and history. The second movement (lines 6–9) asserting identities, has no tense or verb in the Kannada original, though one has to use the verb *to be* in the English translation for such equations, e.g., 'My legs are pillars'; Kannada has only 'My legs themselves, pillars'. The polarities are lined up and judged:

the rich	:	the poor
temple	:	body
make	:	be
the standing (sthāvara)	:	the moving (jaṅgama)

The sthāvara/jaṅgama contrast is not merely an opposition of thing and person. The Vīraśaiva trinity consists of guru, liṅga, and jaṅgama – the spiritual teacher, the symbolic stone-emblem of Śiva, and His wandering mendicant representative. They are three yet one. Basavaṇṇa insists, in another poem, 'sthāvara and jaṅgama are one' to the truly worshipful spirit. Yet if a devotee prefer external worship of the stone liṅga (sthāvara) to serving a human jaṅgama, he would be worthy of scorn.

Jaṅgama in the last sentence of the poem is in the neuter (jaṅgamakke). This makes it an abstraction, raising the particular living/dying Jaṅgama to a universal immortal principle. But the word jaṅgama also carries its normal association of 'holy person', thus including the Living and the Living-forever.

VACANAS AND HINDUISM

Anthropologists like Robert Redfield and Milton Singer speak of 'great' and 'little' traditions in Indian civilization; other pairs of terms have been proposed: popular/learned, folk/classical, low/high, parochial/universal, peasant/aristocratic, lay/hieratic. The native Indian tradition speaks of *mārga* ('classical') and *deśi* ('folk'). The several pairs capture different aspects of a familiar dichotomy, though none of them is satisfactory or definitive. We shall use 'great' and 'little' here as convenient labels. Reservations regarding the concepts and the dichotomy will appear below.

The 'great' tradition in India would be inter-regional, pan-Indian; its vehicle, Sanskrit. The 'little' tradition would consist of many regional traditions, carried by the regional languages. It should not be forgotten that many of the regional languages and cultures themselves, e.g., Tamil, have long traditions, divisible into 'ancient' and 'modern' historically, 'classical' and 'folk' or 'high' and 'low' synchronically. Such languages have a formal 'high' style and many informal colloquial 'low' dialects. These colloquial dialects may be either social or sub-regional. Cultural traditions too tend to be organized similarly into related yet distinct sub-cultures socially and regionally. Even the so-called 'great' tradition is not as monolithic as it is often assumed to be. Still, taken in the large, one may speak of pan-Indian Sanskritic 'great' traditions and many regional 'little' traditions. But traditions are not divided by impermeable membranes; they interflow into one another, responsive to differences of density as in an osmosis. It is often difficult to isolate elements as belonging exclusively to the one or the other.

A Sanskrit epic like the *Mahābhārata* contains in its encyclopedic range much folk material, like tales, beliefs, proverbs, picked obviously from folk sources, refurbished, Sanskritized, fixed forever in the Sanskritic artifice of eternity. But in a profoundly oral culture like the Indian, the Sanskrit *Mahābhārata* itself gets returned to the oral folk-traditions, contributing the transformed materials back to the 'little' traditions to be further diffused and diffracted. It gets 'translated' from the Sanskrit into the regional languages; in the course of the 'translations', the regional poet infuses it with his rich local traditions, combining not only the pan-Indian 'great' with the regional 'little', but the regional 'great' with the regional 'little' traditions as well. Thus many cycles of give-and-take are set in motion. Such interaction and exchange is well expressed in the following parable of the transposed heads:

A sage's wife, Māriamma, was sentenced by her husband to death. At the moment of execution she embraced an outcaste woman, Ellamma, for her sympathy. In the fray both the outcaste woman and the brahmin lost their heads. Later, the husband relented, granted them pardon and restored their heads by his spiritual powers. But the heads were transposed by mistake. To Māriamma (with a brahmin head and an outcaste body) goats and cocks but not buffaloes were sacrificed; to Ellamma (outcaste head and brahmin body) buffaloes instead of goats and cocks.

According to Whitehead's *Village Gods of South India*, the legend probably represents the fusion of the Aryan and Dravidian cults in the days when the Aryan culture first found its way into (South) India. It could stand just as well for transpositions in the 'great' and 'little' traditions.

For the sake of exposition we may speak of several parallel components in the 'great' and 'little' traditions in Hinduism. We may consider these under four tentative heads: (a) social organization, (b) text, (c) performance, (d) mythology. For the 'great' traditions they would be respectively, (a) the caste hierarchy, (b) the Vedas, (c) the Vedic rituals, (d) the pan-Indian pantheon of Viṣṇu, Śiva, Indra etc.

We may recognize elements parallel to these four for the 'little' traditions. Instead of the Vedic texts there would be *purāṇas*, saints' legends, minor mythologies, systems of magic and superstition – often composed in the regional languages. These are mostly local traditions, though they may seek, and often find, prestige by being re-written in Sanskrit and absorbed into the pan-Indian corpus. Parallel to the Vedic rituals, every village has its own particular kinds of 'cultural performance' – local animal sacrifices, magical practices, wakes, vigils, fairs. The social organization of the 'little' traditions would be the local sects and cults; the mythology would centre round regional deities, worship of stone, trees, crossroads and rivers. (See diagram on page 34.)

Vacanas are *bhakti* poems, poems of personal devotion to a god, often a particular form of the god. The vacana saints reject not only the 'great' traditions of Vedic religion, but the 'little' local traditions as well. They not only scorn the effectiveness of the Vedas as scripture; they reject the little legends of the local gods and goddesses. The first of the following examples mocks at orthodox ritual genuflections and recitations; the second, at animal sacrifice in folk-religion:

See-saw watermills bow their heads.
So what?
Do they get to be devotees
to the Master?

The tongs join hands.
So what?
Can they be humble in service
to the Lord?

Parrots recite.
So what?
Can they read the Lord?

How can the slaves of the Bodiless God,
Desire,
  know the way
  our Lord's Men move
  or the stance of their standing?

BASAVAṆṆA 125

The sacrificial lamb brought for the festival
ate up the green leaf brought for the decorations.

Not knowing a thing about the kill,
it wants only to fill its belly:
born that day, to die that day.

But tell me:
did the killers survive,
O lord of the meeting rivers?

BASAVAṆṆA 129

Religions set apart certain times and places as specially sacred: rituals and worship are performed at appointed times, pilgrimages are undertaken to well-known holy places. There is a holy map as well as a holy calendar. If you die in Benares, sinner though you are, you will go straight to heaven. The following vacana represents the contempt of the saint for all sacred space and sacred time:

To the utterly at-one with Śiva
there's no dawn,
no new moon,
no noonday,
nor equinoxes,
nor sunsets,
nor full moons;

his front yard
is the true Benares,

O Rāmanātha.

DĀSIMAYYA 98

In his protest against traditional dichotomies, he rejects also the differences between man and woman as superficial:

If they see
breasts and long hair coming
they call it woman,

if beard and whiskers
they call it man:

but, look, the self that hovers
in between
is neither man
nor woman

O Rāmanātha

DĀSIMAYYA 133

The Vīraśaiva saints – unlike exponents of other kinds of Hinduism, and like other bhakti movements of India – do not believe that religion is something one is born with or into. An orthodox Hindu believes a Hindu is born, not made. With such a belief, there is no place for conversion in Hinduism; a man born to his caste or faith cannot choose and change, nor can others change him. But if he believes in acquiring merit only by living and believing certain things, then there is room for choosing and changing his beliefs. He can then convert and be converted. If, as these saints believed, he also believes that his god is the true god, the only true god, it becomes imperative to convert the misguided and bring light to the benighted. Missions are born. Bhakti religions proselytize, unlike classical Hinduism. Some of the incandescence of Vīraśaiva poetry is the white heat of truth-seeing and truth-saying in a dark deluded world; their monotheism lashes out in an atmosphere of animism and polytheism.[4]

4. In the light of these considerations, it is not surprising that Christian missionaries were greatly attracted to South Indian bhakti texts and traditions, often translated them, speculated that bhakti attitudes were the result of early Christian influence. Also, Christian texts and lives (especially the New Testament, and the lives of saints) strike many Hindus as variants of bhakti.

How can I feel right
  about a god who eats up lacquer and melts,
  who wilts when he sees fire?

How can I feel right
  about gods you sell in your need,

  and gods you bury for fear of thieves?

The lord of the meeting rivers,
self-born, one with himself,

he alone is the true god.

BASAVAṆṆA 558

The pot is a god. The winnowing
fan is a god. The stone in the
street is a god. The comb is a
god. The bowstring is also a
god. The bushel is a god and the
spouted cup is a god.

Gods, gods, there are so many
there's no place left
for a foot.
  There is only
one god. He is our Lord
of the Meeting Rivers.

BASAVAṆṆA 563

The crusading militancy at the heart of bhakti[5] makes it double-edged, bisexual, as expressed in poems like the following:

Look here, dear fellow:
I wear these men's clothes
only for you.

Sometimes I am man,
sometimes I am woman.

O lord of the meeting rivers
I'll make war for you
but I'll be your devotees' bride.

BASAVAṆṆA 703

THE 'UNMEDIATED VISION'

Why did the vacanakāras (and certain other bhakti traditions in India and elsewhere) reject, at least in their more intense moods, the 'great' and 'little' traditions? I think it is because the 'great' and 'little' traditions, as we have described them, together constitute 'establishment' in the several senses of the word. They *are* the establishment, the stable, the secure,

5. The vacanas often divide the world of men between *bhakta* (devotee) and *bhavi* (worldling), men of faith and the infidels – reminiscent of Christian/Heathen, Jew/Gentile, divisions. One amusing legend speaks of a Śaiva saint who lived in the world, devoting his energies to converting worldlings to the Śaiva faith – by any means whatever: bribes, favours, love, and if needed physical force, coercing or persuading them to wear the Śaiva emblem of holy ash on the forehead. One day, Śiva himself came down in disguise to see him. But he did not recognize Śiva and proceeded to convert him, offering him holy ash, trying to force it on him when he seemed reluctant. When his zeal became too oppressive, Śiva tried in vain to tell him who he was, but was forced down on his knees for the baptism of ash – even Śiva had to become a Śaiva.

the sthāvara, in the social sense. In another sense, such traditions symbolize man's attempt to establish or stabilize the universe for himself. Such traditions wish to render the universe manipulable, predictable, safe. Every prescribed ritual or magical act has given results. These are spelled out in clear terms in a *phalaśruti*.[6]

Ritual, superstition, sacred space and sacred time, pilgrimage and temple-going, offerings to god and priest, prayers and promises – all forms of 'making' and 'doing' – all of them are performed to get results, to manipulate and manage carefully the Lord's universe to serve one's own purposes, to save one's soul or one's skin. Salvation, like prosperity, has a price. It can be paid – by oneself or by proxy. The 'great' and 'little' traditions organize and catalogue the universe, and make available the price-list.

But the vacanakāras have a horror of such bargains, such manipulations, the arrogance of such predictions. The Lord's world is unpredictable, and all predictions are false, ignorant, and worse.

Thus, classical belief systems, social customs and superstitions (Basavaṇṇa 581, 105), image worship (Basavaṇṇa 558), the caste system (Dāsimayya 96), the Vedic ritual of *yajña* (Basavaṇṇa 125), as well as local sacrifices of lambs and goats (Basavaṇṇa 129) – all of them are fiercely questioned and ridiculed.

Vacanas often go further and reject the idea of doing good so that one may go to heaven. Righteousness, virtue, being correct, doing the right things, carry no guarantee to god.

6. A *phalaśruti* is 'an account of the merit which accrues through a religous act. For pilgrimage, it is of the general form "the place of x . . . when visited at the time . . . together with the performance of observance a, b, c, d, . . . yields the following results"; they are almost always both secular and religious, as the curing of a disease and securing a better existence in the next life.' Agehananda Bharati, 'Pilgrimage in the Indian Tradition', in *History of Religions*, vol. 3, no. 1, p. 145.

One may note here again that making and doing are both opposed to being or knowing (in a non-discursive sense).

Feed the poor
tell the truth
make water-places
and build tanks for a town –

you may then go to heaven
after death, but you'll get nowhere
near the truth of our Lord

And the man who knows our Lord,
he gets no results.

ALLAMA 959

All true experience of god is *kṛpa*, grace that cannot be called, recalled, or commanded. The vacanas distinguish *anubhava* 'experience', and *anubhāva* 'the Experience'. The latter is a search for the 'unmediated vision', the unconditioned act, the unpredictable experience. Living in history, time and cliché, one lives in a world of the pre-established, through the received (*śruti*) and the remembered (*smṛti*). But the Experience when it comes, comes like a storm to all such husks and labels. In a remarkable use of the well-known opportunist proverb ('Winnow when the wind blows'), Chowḍayya the Ferryman says:

Winnow, winnow!
Look here, fellows
winnow when the wind blows.

Remember, the winds
are not in your hands,

Remember, you cannot say
I'll winnow, I'll winnow
tomorrow.

When the winds of the Lord's grace
lash,
quickly, quickly winnow, winnow,
said our Chowḍayya of the Ferrymen.

CHOWḌAYYA OF THE FERRYMEN

A mystical opportunist can only wait for it, be prepared to catch It as It passes. The grace of the Lord is nothing he can invoke or wheedle by prayer, rule, ritual, magical word or sacrificial offering.[7] In *anubhāva* he needs nothing, he is

7. Though the saints generally reject external ceremony the Vīraśaivas have developed their own ceremony and symbols; but they are nothing elaborate like the Vedic. Vīraśaiva orthodoxy depends on the eight coverings or emblems, the aṣṭāvaraṇa. Some of the vacanas mention these, but they are clearly secondary, and mere literal observance of these will not make one a bhakta.

i. The guru or the spiritual guide leads the soul to Śiva.

ii. The liṅga, the only symbol of Śiva, is to be worn inseparably on his body by the devotee. There is no suggestion in any of the known vacanas that the liṅga was a phallic symbol. The Liṅga is Śiva himself, externalized as a form by the guru.

iii. The jaṅgama is a travelling religious teacher, ideally free and pure. To the Vīraśaivas the jaṅgama is the lord on earth, as liṅga and guru are other aspects of Him. The jaṅgama also represents the community of saints, for which every vacanakāra thirsts.

iv. The pādōdaka is the holy water from the feet of the guru, imbibed by the devotee as a mark of his devotion. All things are sanctified by guru, liṅga and jaṅgama.

Nothing; for to be someone, or something, is to be differentiated and separate from God. When he is one with him, he is the Nothing without names. Yet we must not forget that this fierce rebellion against petrification was a rebellion only against contemporary Hindu practice; the rebellion was a call to return to experience. Like European Protestants, the Vīraśaivas returned to what they felt was the original inspiration of the ancient traditions no different from true and present experience.

Defiance is not discontinuity. Alienation from the immediate environment can mean continuity with an older ideal. Protest can take place in the very name of one's opponents' ideals.

We should also remember that the vacana ideals were not all implemented in the Vīraśaiva community; the relation of ideals to realization, the city of god and the city of man, is a complex relation, and we shall not embark here on an

---

v. The prasāda, or 'favour', is signified by food consecrated by the touch of the guru. In Hinduism privilege of food and drink mark and separate caste from caste, male from female, the pure from the polluted. Ideally, pādōdaka and prasāda unite the devotees through commensality and companionship, whatever be their rank, sect or occupation. Such identity and equality are achieved by bhakti to the guru. Note also the importance of water in the ritual, unlike the Vedic fires.

vi. The vibhūti is holy ash prepared by a man of virtue and learning according to elaborate rules, to the accompaniment of sacred chants. Ash is also associated with Śiva, the ascetic who covered His body with it.

vii. The rudrākṣa, 'the eyes of Śiva', are seeds sacred to all Śiva-worshippers, strung into necklaces, bracelets and prayer beads.

viii. The mantra, a sacred formula of five syllables (pañcākṣarā: Namas-Śivāya 'Obeisance to Śiva'), is the King of Mantras, the only one accepted by the Vīraśaivas. According to all Śaivas, these five syllables are 'far weightier than the 70 million other mantras put together'. S. C. Nandimath, *A Handbook of Vīraśaivism*, p. 63.

anthropology[8] of contemporary Lingayat community, for it would require no less to describe the texts in context.

What we have said so far may be summarized in a chart. The dotted lines indicate the 'permeable membranes' that allow transfusion.

HINDUISM

STRUCTURE | ANTI-STRUCTURE

	STRUCTURE		ANTI-STRUCTURE
	Establishment: 'Public' Religion		*Protest: 'Personal' Religion*
	Great Tradition	Little Tradition	
Text	Vedas etc.	Local Purānas etc.	
Performance	Vedic ritual	Local sacrifices etc.	*v.* Bhakti
Social organization	Caste-hierarchy	Sects and cults	
Mythology	Pan-Indian deities	Regional deities	

Following Victor Turner in *The Ritual Process*, I am using the terms structure and anti-structure. I would further distinguish between anti-structure and counter-structure. Anti-

8. cf. L. Dumont's *Homo Hierarchicus*, Chicago, 1970. See also W. McCormack's anthropological appendix to this work.

structure is anti- 'structure', ideological rejection of the idea of structure itself. Yet bhakti-communities, while proclaiming anti-structure, necessarily develop their own structures for behaviour and belief, often minimal, frequently composed of elements selected from the very structures they deny or reject. The Vīraśaiva saints developed in their community, not a full-scale 'Communitas' of equal beings – but a three-part hierarchy, based not on birth or occupation, but on mystical achievement: the Guru, the Elders, and the Novices. (Poems like Mahādēvi 45, 60, 77 celebrate this mystical hierarchy.) The saints are drawn from every social class, caste and trade, touchable and untouchable – from kings and ministers to manual workers – laundrymen, boatmen, leatherworkers. Such collapsing of classes and occupations in the new community of saints and saints-to-be, however short-lived, led to Vīraśaiva slogans like *kāyakavē kailāsa* (Basavaṇṇa), 'Work is heaven', 'to work is to be in the Lord's Kingdom'. Kāyaka could also mean the work of ritual or other worship; here I think it means 'labour, work'. Furthermore, in the new community, instead of the multiple networks of normal social relationships, we have face-to-face dyadic relations with each other, with the guru, especially with God. Such dyads are symbolized by intimate relationships: lover/beloved, father/son, mother/child, whore/customer, master/man (e.g., Basavaṇṇa 62, 70, 97 etc.).

There are many varieties of bhakti;[9] here we refer only to the kind exemplified by the vacanas. In the Northern

9. Two kinds are broadly distinguished: *nirguṇa* and *saguṇa*. Nirguṇa bhakti is personal devotion offered to an impersonal attributeless godhead (nirguṇa), without 'body, parts or passion'; though he may bear a name like Śiva, he does not have a mythology, he is not the Śiva of mythology. By and large, the Vīraśaiva saints are nirguṇa bhaktas, relating personally and passionately to the Infinite Absolute. Saguṇa bhakti is bhakti for a particular god with attributes (saguṇa), like Krishna. The woman saint Mahādēviyakka, in this selection, comes

traditions, Kabir's poems would be a parallel example. The 'great' and the 'little' traditions flow one into the other, as in an osmosis. They together constitute the 'public religion' of Hinduism, its 'establishment' or 'structure' as defined above. Bhakti as anti-structure begins by denying and defying such an establishment; but in course of time, the heretics are canonized; temples are erected to them, Sanskrit hagiographies are composed about them. Not only local legend and ritual, but an elaborate theology assimilating various 'great tradition' elements may grow around them. They become, in retrospect, founders of a new caste, and are defied in turn by new egalitarian movements.

Vīraśaivas were protesters not only against the Hinduism of their time, but also against Jainism, the powerful competitor to Hinduism. Basavaṇṇa's and Dāsimayya's lives were desperate struggles against both Brahminism and Jainism.The jainas were politically powerful in the area and represented privilege. Ideologically, their belief in *karma* was absolute; the individual had inexorably to run through the entire chain of action and consequence, with no glimmer of grace. To this absolute determinism, the Vīraśaiva saints opposed their sense of grace and salvation through bhakti. Yet they shared with Jainism and Buddhism the doctrine of *ahimsa* or non-violence towards all creation (cf. Dasarēśwara, p. 54), the abhorrence of animal sacrifice and ritual orthodoxy. Śaivism in general, and Vīraśaivism even more so, has been rightly described as 'a revolt from within, while Buddhism and Jainism were revolts from the outside'. (Nandimath, p. 53.)

---

close to being a good example, though not a full-blown one – for she speaks little of the mythological or other attributes of Śiva, say, his divine consort Pārvati or his mythic battles with evil demons. Yet she is in love with him, her sensuality is her spiritual metaphor. Vaiṣṇava bhakti, bhakti for Krishna or Rāma, generally offer the best examples of saguṇa bhakti.

Some Vīraśaivas, however, disclaim all connections with Hinduism.

THE VACANA FORM AND ORAL POETICS

The Sanskrit religious texts are described as *śruti* and *smṛti*. *Smṛti* is what is remembered, what is memorable; *śruti*, what is heard, what is received. Vīraśaiva saints called their compositions *vacana*, or 'what is said'. *Vacana*, as an active mode, stands in opposition to both *śruti* and *smṛti*: not what is heard, but what is said; not remembered or received, but uttered here and now. To the saints, religion is not a spectator sport, a reception, a consumption; it is an experience of Now, a way of being. This distinction is expressed in the language of the vacanas, the forms the vacanas take. Though medieval Kannada was rich in native Dravidian metres, and in borrowed Sanskritic forms, no metrical line or stanza is used in the vacanas.[10] The saints did not follow any of these models. Basavaṇṇa said:

> I don't know anything like timebeats and metre
> nor the arithmetic of strings and drums;
>
> I don't know the count of iamb and dactyl.
> My lord of the meeting rivers,
> as nothing will hurt you
> I'll sing as I love.
>
> BASAVAṆṆA 949

It is not even he that sings; the Lord sings through him.

10. One of the general meanings of 'vacana' is 'prose'. The vacanakāras did not think of themselves as poets, for Poetry (poesy?) too is part of court and temple and punditry, part of sthāvara.

The instrument is not what is 'made', but what one 'is'. The body can be lute as it can be temple.

> Make of my body the beam of a lute
> of my head the sounding gourd
> of my nerves the strings
> of my fingers the plucking rods.
>
> Clutch me close
> and play your thirty-two songs
> O lord of the meeting rivers!
>
> BASAVAṆṆA 500

The vacana is thus a rejection of premeditated art, the sthāvaras of form. It is not only a spontaneous cry but a cry for spontaneity – for the music of a body given over to the Lord.

The traditional time-beat, like the ritual gesture, was felt to be learned, passive, inorganic; too well organized to be organic. Here too, the sthāvara, the standing thing, shall fall, but the jaṅgama shall prevail. The battles that were fought in Europe under the banners of Classical/Romantic, rhetoric/sincerity, impersonal/personal, metre/*vers libre* were fought in Indian literature in genres like the vacana.

But then 'spontaneity' has its own rhetorical structure; no free verse is truly free. Without a repertoire of structures to rely on, there can be no spontaneity. In the free-seeming verse, there are always patterns that loom and withdraw, figures of sound that rhyme and ring bells with the figures of meaning. It is not surprising that M. Cidānanda Murti[11] has shown how the apparently metreless metre of the vacanas has a *tripadi*-base. *Tripadi* is a popular 3-line form of the oral tradition used widely both in folk song and in folk epigram.

11. In a Kannada article published in his *Saṁsōdhana taraṅga*, Mysore, 1966, pp. 190–204.

Scholars like Parry and Lord have studied the techniques of oral verse-making in folk-epics. They have paid little attention to shorter forms. Several features noted for heroic oral poetry do appear in the vacanas: in particular a common stock of themes that occur in changing forms, repetitions of phrases and ideas, the tendency to cycles or sequences of poems. But the extensive use of formulae and substitutes in the strict sense and a distinct given prosody, both characteristic of the oral bardic traditions, are generally absent in the vacana, a genre of epigram and lyric.

The vacanakāras, however, did use stock phrases, proverbs, and religious commonplaces of the time. This stock, shared by Southern and Northern saints, the Upaniṣads and the folk alike, included figures, symbols and paradoxes often drawn from an ancient and pan-Indian pool of symbology. Bhakti saints, like the vacanakāras, have been called the 'great integrators',[12] bringing the high to the low, esoteric paradox to the man in the street, transmuting ancient and abstruse ideas into live contemporary experiences; at the same time, finding everyday symbols for the timeless.

They also travelled within and across regions, claimed kindred saints of other regions in their geneological tree of gurus. Thus the Vīraśaiva saints named the 63 Tamil Saints among their forebears. Śaivism knits faraway Kashmir with South India, and within South India the saints of Tamil, Kannada and Telugu. Both Kābir of the Hindi region,

12. See V. Raghavan, *The Great Integrators: the Saint-singers of India*, Delhi, 1966, for a discussion of saints from other regions, as well as their relation to each other and the Indian heritage. Here, we omit other parallels of, and influences on bhakti, like the Muslim Sufi mystics, the esoteric cults of tantra and yoga in their Hindu, Buddhist and Jaina versions. Nor can we consider here the gifts of bhakti poets to modern India, in poetry (e.g. Tagore in Bengal, Bharati in Tamil); in politics (Gandhi), religion and philosophy (Sri Ramakrishna and Sri Aurobindo).

and Caitanya of Bengal, were inspired by southern precedents. Chronologically from the seventh century on, century after century, bhakti movements have arisen in different regions and languages, spanning the whole Indian sub-continent, in Tamil, Kannada, Marathi, Gujerati, Hindi, Bengali, Assamese, and Punjabi, roughly in that order. Like a lit fuse, the passion of bhakti seems to spread from region to region, from century to century, quickening the religious impulse. Arising in particular regions, speaking the local spoken languages, it is yet inter-regional – both 'parochial' and 'universal'. Even modern urban bhakti groups include in their hymnals, songs of several languages and ages.

So it is not surprising that

> from the Upaniṣads onwards, a large number of similes and analogies have been pressed into service, 'the Seed and the Tree, the Sea and the Rivers, the Spider and its Self-woven web, the Thread and the Gems, the Warp and the Woof, the River and the Boat, the Chariot and the Charioteer, the King and his Subjects, the Child and its fantasies, the Stage and Acting, the Puppet and Puppeteer, the Dream, the Dance, and the Sport (Līlā)'.[13]

To take a few examples: see Mahādēviyakka 17 for the Spider and its self-woven Web (as silkworm and cocoon), 20 for the puppet at the end of a string; Basavaṇṇa 8 for the Sea of Life, 33 for the mind as monkey; 144 for the river and the sea.

Yet it should not be imagined that the common stock was used in exactly similar ways. Only the components were the same; the functions, the emerging meanings, were often startlingly different. For instance, the image of the insect weaving a web out of its body is an ancient one. The *Bṛhadāraṇyaka Upaniṣad* has this description of Brahman, the creator:

13. Raghavan, op. cit., p. 37.

As a spider emerges (from itself) by
(spinning) threads [out of its own body] . . .
so too from this self do all the life-breaths,
all the worlds, all the gods, and all contin-
gent beings rise up in all directions.[14]

Mahādēviyakka/ has the following:

Like a silkworm weaving
her house with love
from her marrow,
                    and dying
in her body's threads
winding tight, round
and round,
          I burn
desiring what the heart desires.

Cut through, O lord,
my heart's greed,
and show me
your way out,

O lord white as jasmine.

MAHĀDĒVIYAKKA 17

Note the startling difference in the feeling-tone of these passages, the coolness of the Upaniṣad and the woman-saint's heart-rending cry for release. The classical text describes the object, the Cosmic creator; the vacana describes the subject, the speaker's feelings towards herself. The one describes creation by and out of the creator; the other describes the self trammelled in its self-created illusions. One speaks of the birth of worlds, awesome, wondrous, non-human; the other speaks of a death, small, calling for compassion, all too human.

Though Basavaṇṇa says in the poem quoted earlier,

14. II-1.20 trans. R. C. Zaehner, *Hindu Scriptures*, New York, 1966, p. 44.

'I'll sing as I love,' rejecting conventional patterns of verse-making, the vacanas evolve a distinctive structure (as, in the religious dimension, anti-structure develops a counter-structure). Their metre is not syllabic but syntactic; the regularities and returning units are not usually units of sound, but units of syntax and semantics. The oral origins of the poetry are clear in its favourite structure. The poetics of the vacana is an oral poetics.

'Grammatical parallelism[15] belongs to the poetic canon of numerous folk-patterns,' says Roman Jakobson. He also cites work on parallelisms in Vedic, Chinese, Finnish and notably Hebrew verse. While this is no place to undertake a full technical analysis, it is necessary to indicate a few major symmetries and patterns in vacana poetry and their function.

A simple-looking poem like the following has many symmetries:

1. The master of the house, is he at home, or isn't he?
2. Grass on the threshold,
3. dirt in the house:

4. The master of the house, is he at home, or isn't he?
5. Lies in the body,
6. lust in the heart:

7. no, the master of the house is not at home,
8. our Lord of the Meeting Rivers.

BASAVAṆṆA 97

English syntax does not allow a natural and succinct translation of all these symmetries. A literal translation will indicate some of them, including the actual word repetitions, and suggest the departures that the present translation has made from the original:

15. Roman Jakobson, 'Grammatical parallelism and its Russian facet', *Language*, Vol. 42.2 (1966), pp. 399–420.

1. *maneyoḷage maneyoḍeyaniddānō illavō?*
2. *hostilalli hullu huṭṭi,*
3. *maneyoḷage raja tumbi,*
4. *maneyoḷage maneyoḍeyaniddānō illavō?*
5. *tanuvoḷage husi tumbi,*
6. *manadoḷage viṣaya tuṁbi,*
7. *maneyoḷage maneyoḍeyanillā,*
8. *kūḍalasaṅgama dēvā*[16]

The literal translation is as follows, with parallel grammatical constructions indicated by letters (A, B, C, D, a, b, c); similarly structured 'metrical' lines by roman numerals (I, II, II):

A B C D
1. I house-inside house-master is-he, or is-he-not?

a b c
2. II threshold-on grass having-grown,

a b c
3. II house-inside dust having-filled

A B C D
4. I house-inside house-master is-he, or is-he-not?

a b c
5. II body-inside lies having-filled,

a b c
6. II heart-inside carnal-desires having-filled,

A B C
7. I house-inside house-master is-not

8. III Meeting-of-Rivers God

16. We must remember that all the line-divisions are arbitrary. Though editors make their own 'cuts' according to syntax, the original manuscript has no indication of line-, phrase- or word-division, nor punctuation. Note also the absence of distinctions like house/home; both are *mane* in Kannada.

For instance, lines 1 and 4 are simple repetitions, enclosing 2 and 3 which use the same basic phrase pattern in the Kannada original:

2. hostilalli hullu huṭṭi: threshold-on grass having-grown
3. maneyoḷage raja tumbi: house-inside dust having-filled

The syntactic construction is the same, but the slots are filled with different words.

Lines 5 and 6, like 2 and 3 use the same syntactic construction but the words are chosen from entirely different semantic domains: body and mind. Because the syntax is the same in 2, 3 and 5, 6, a metaphoric ratio is created by the parallelism:

threshold: house:: body: heart

Line 7, 'The master of the house is not at home' repeats the construction in 1 and 4, with a difference: 1 and 4 are questions, and 7 is the answer to it. (cf. the original and the literal translation above.)

The last line 'Lord of the Meeting Rivers' is the regular signature-line which appears in poem after poem – a singular line with no parallels within the poem but repeated as a refrain across poems: it has the effect of binding together into a cycle all the poems of the saint. Further, the signature-line, though repeated in every poem, does not have everywhere the same vocative function. For instance in poem 97, it is ambiguous: it is both an address to the lord, and an attribute of 'the master of the house'; so that the whole poem is about the absence of the Lord of the Meeting Rivers in the heart of the devotee. As elsewhere in parallelistic texts (e.g., Vedic Sanskrit, Chinese, Russian, Biblical Hebrew) 'the occasional isolated single lines' chiefly signal the beginning or the end of an entire text or its paragraphs.[17]

But the repetitions or parallelisms are also ordered towards

17. Jakobson, op. cit., p. 409.

a crescendo. In the above poem, it is a climax of denial. In Basavaṇṇa 563 (quoted on p. 28) after a disgusted crescendo listing of 'the pot is a god. The winnowing/fan is a god. The stone in the street is a god etc.', there is a climax of assertion: 'There is only/one god. He is our Lord/of the Meeting Rivers.' Sometimes there are inverse parallels – a 'chiasm': in 105, 'a snake-charmer and his noseless wife' meet head-on 'a noseless woman/and her snake-charming husband' – the inversion representing the mirror-effect of this encounter with the Self as the Other.

In Mahādēvi 336, the three central images are parallel constructions, each therefore a metaphor for the other and all of them approximations to a description of the lord's perfect love. But the three metaphors (arrow, embrace, welding), chosen from three different semantic areas, are also a progression, three phases of love as well as the act of love.

Repetition of word and construction, repetitions with a difference, combined with progressions towards a climax of assertion or reversal are devices of oral composition. These carry with them a number of paired opposites or lexical partners which appear in similar syntactic positions; they imply each other, they negate each other; they are often held together as a pair by rhyme or alliteration (e.g., liṅga/aṅga).

As shown earlier, a poem like 820 is built around several pairs of such oppositions: temple/body (*dēha/dēgula*), sthāvara/jaṅgama. Some of the other pairs are body/mind (B. 36), creature/creator, the faithful/the unbeliever (*bhakta/bhavi*), lord/human soul (liṅga/aṅga), other gods/Śiva (quoted on p. 19).

The oral origins and qualities of this poetry are demonstrated and reinforced by the never-failing vigorous tones of speech, the imperatives (Basavaṇṇa 162), instructions (500, quoted on p. 38), warnings (212), pleas (350), curses (639), questions and answers (97), oaths (430), vocatives (848), outcries (8), chatty talk (703) and the recurring invocation to Śiva, the eternal addressee.

Linguistically too, the vacana-poets were the first to use the changing local sub-standard spoken dialects of their birth-places in poetry, while contemporary poets wrote in a highly stylized archaic language, preferring again the jaṅgamas of language to the sthāvaras. In fact vacanas and inscriptions are the most important witnesses to the dialectal speech of medieval Kannada country. In their urgency and need for directness, they defied standard upper-class educated speech and stylized metrical literary genres, as they defied ritual and orthodoxy. Such untrammelled speech in poetry has a fresh 'modern' ring to it in imagery, rhythm and idiom – a freedom that modern literary writers in Kannada have not yet quite won.

The common language of the vacanas did not exclude Sanskrit words (and even common Sanskrit quotations); instead the vacanakāras used Sanskrit with brilliant and complex effects of contrast, setting it off against the native dialectal Kannada. To take one instance, Mahādēvi 17 (quoted on p. 41) opens with the sentence:

teraṇiyahuḷu tanna snēhadinda maneya māḍi tanna
nūlu tannanē sutti sutti sāva teranante

Like a silkworm weaving
her house with love
from her marrow,
                    and dying
in her body's threads
winding tight, round
and round . . .

In that Kannada clause, there is only one Sanskrit-derived word *snēha*, meaning in common usage 'friendship, fondness, love, any attachment'; but etymologically it means 'sticky substance' like oil or marrow (in my translation of the untranslatable I have tried to suggest both by 'love' and 'marrow'). The word stands out (like the Greek/Latin in Shakespeare's Anglo-Saxon) gathering double meanings to itself. The sticky substance out of which the worm weaves its threads, as well as the attachments in which humans trammel themselves, are suggested and inter-related in one stroke by the word *snēha*. Furthermore, here as elsewhere in the vacanas, the use of Sanskrit itself becomes symbolic, symbolic of abstraction. The god's names are partly Sanskrit: e.g., in Cennamallikārjuna, *cenna* 'lovely' is Kannada, the rest Sanskrit. But, because of the transparent Kannada, the Sanskrit too is never opaque or distant for long; it becomes double-faced as in the case of *snēha* above, by etymological recovery: even linguistically the Body stirs in the Temple. The etymologies of the Sanskrit names are never far from the surface, and often participate in the poetry. The proper name Guhēsvara 'Lord of Caves' is appropriate to Allama: his favourite imagery is of dark and light (e.g., 219, on p. 154). Mallikārjuna ('Arjuna, Lord of goddess Mallikā' – the god's name including His beloved – or literally, 'Lord White as Jasmine'), is appropriate to Mahādēvi whose metaphor is love itself, and who is ever thrilled by the lord's beauty. Rāmanātha, or Śiva as worshipped by Rāma as his lord, is right for Dāsimayya who urges the greatness of Śiva over all other gods. With his water-imagery (cf. 8) and themes of merging social differences, Basavaṇṇa's god is Kūḍalasaṅgamadēva, the Lord of the Meeting Rivers. Interestingly enough, the last name combines in itself both Kannada (kūḍalu, 'meeting of rivers') and Sanskrit (saṅgama, synonymous with kūḍalu). Such quickening of etymologies in the poetry is one reason for translating attributive proper names into literal English – hoping that by using them constantly as a repetitive formula they will keep their chanting refrain quality and work as unique proper names.

THE 'LANGUAGE OF SECRECY' (SANDHYĀBHĀSA)

The rangē of vacana expression spans a pan-Indian stock of figures, homely images of everyday experience, the sense and idiom of the earth, as well as an abstruse esoteric symbolism. The esoteric vacanas are called *beḍagina vacana* (fancy poems), more riddle than poem and, oftentimes, with a whole occult glossary for key. This glossary is made up of a common pool of symbols and concepts drawn from yogic psychology and tantric philosophy. Allamaprabhu, the most metaphysical of the vacanakāras, has many *beḍagina* vacanas, and we have included a few. For instance, Allama 218:

> They don't know the day
> is the dark's face,
> and dark the day's.
>
> A necklace of nine jewels
> lies buried, intact, in the face of the night;
> in the face of day a tree
> with leaves of nine designs.
>
> When you feed the necklace
> to the tree,
> the Breath enjoys it
> in the Lord of the Caves.

The paradoxical images of this poem have a surrealist brilliance in themselves. To a learned Vīraśaiva, the poem would mean the following:

The night and day are obviously ignorance and awareness. It is in the experience of the ignorant that we find the jewel of wisdom, a necklace of nine liṅgas. In awareness is knowledge and discrimination (the tree), carefully nurtured. But only when the wisdom of the ignorant experience is fed to the discrimination of the aware, the Liṅga of the Breath finds true joy.

Such a dark, ambiguous language of ciphers (*sandhyābhāṣa* or 'intentional language') has been much discussed by scholars of Yoga and tantra.[18] Riddles and enigmas were used even in Vedic times. In the heterodox and esoteric cults, such systems of cryptography were intended to conceal the secret doctrine from the uninitiated and the outsider. But riddle and paradox are also meant to shatter the ordinary language of ordinary experiences, baffling the rational intelligence to look through the glass darkly till it begins to see. (Just as often, it may degenerate into a mere mental gymnastic.) It is 'a process of destroying and reinventing language' till we find ourselves in 'a universe of analogies, homologies, and double meanings'.[19]

A related device is a favourite with vacanas: extended metaphor, a simile which projects a whole symbolic situation suppressing one part of the comparison, as in Basavaṇṇa 111. One of the most moving uses of the extended analogue is Mahādēviyakka's love of God, where all the phases of love become metaphors for the phases of mystical union and alienation. For instance:

I have Māyā for mother-in-law;
the world for father-in-law;
three brothers-in-law like tigers;

and the husband's thoughts
are full of laughing women:
no god, this man.

And I cannot cross the sister-in-law.

18. cf. Eliade's *Yoga*, pp. 249–54.
19. ibid., p. 251.

But I will
give this wench the slip
and go cuckold my husband with Hara, my lord.

My mind is my maid:
by her kindness, I join
my Lord,
my utterly beautiful Lord
from the mountain-peaks
my lord as white as jasmine

and I will make Him
my good husband.

MAHĀDĒVIYAKKA 328

Mahādēviyakka's poem explicitly takes over conventions of Indian love-poetry (available in Sanskrit as in the regional languages).[20] An abhisārikā, a woman stealing out of a houseful of relatives to meet her lover, is the central image The method is the method of allegory, explicitly equating, one-for-one, various members of a household with various abstractions: Māyā or Primal Illusion is the mother-in-law, the world is the father-in-law. Some of the equations are implicit, and they draw on a common background of philosophical concepts. For instance, the three brothers-in-law are the three *guṇas*, the three ultimate components which make all the particulars of nature what they are; these three are inescapable as long as one is part of nature, they keep a tiger-vigil. The husband is Karma, the past of the ego's many lives. The sister-in-law, who also keeps the speaker imprisoned, is apparently the *vāsanā*, the binding memory

20. Vaiṣṇava bhakti poems make the fullest use of these conventions, especially in the personnel and affairs of Kṛṣṇa and Rādhā. For examples, see *In Praise of Krishna, Songs from the Bengali*, translated by E. D. Dimock and D. Levertov, New York, 1967.

or 'smell' that the Karma-Past carries with it. The kind confidante or maid is the Mind, who alone helps her meet her Lord and keep the tryst.

Note how all the relationships mentioned are those 'made' by marriage. The house is full of in-laws,[21] acquired, social ties. Not one person is related to the woman by birth. (The mother-in-law in a South Indian family of this region could be a blood-relation, a paternal aunt. This only adds a further nuance, the conversion by ritual of a blood-kin into an in-law.) A net of marriage rules and given relations binds her. These are what you make and enter into, not what you are born with. This elaborate build-up of social bonds is shattered by the cuckolding climax of the poem, with the Lord as the adulterous lover. Here a vulgar Kannada word is used to speak of the 'cuckolding', the 'fornication'. The whole poem, written in a colloquial, vigorous speaking style, moves toward the word *hādara* or fornication, enacting by linguistic shock the shock of her explosive desire to shatter the entire framework of so-called legitimacies. Elsewhere also Mahādēviyakka rejects outright all notions of modesty as a virtue. She is supposed to have thrown off her clothes at one point, in defiance of the indecent pruderies of the society around her.

This stresses the view that love of God is not only an unconditional giving up of all, but it is necessarily anti-'structure', an anti-social 'unruly' relationship – unmaking, undoing, the man-made. It is an act of violation against ordinary expected loyalties, a breakdown of the predictable and the secure. Some such notion is at the heart of this complex of metaphoric action. The Lord is the Illicit

21. The English over-emphasizes the 'law' aspects, by its various 'in-law' compounds in the kinship system. Kannada has unitary words for all the 'made' relations: *atte* (mother-in-law), *māva* (father-in-law), etc.

Lover; He will break up the world of Karma and normal relationships, the husband's family that must necessarily be violated and trespassed against, if one should have anything to do with God.

Such a poem is an allegory with no need for a key. Sometimes in the vacanakāra's quest for the unmediated vision, there comes a point when language, logic and metaphor are not enough; at such points, the poet begins with a striking traditional metaphor[22] and denies it at the end:

Looking for your light,
I went out:

it was like the sudden dawn
of a million million suns,

a ganglion of lightnings
for my wonder.

O Lord of Caves,
if you are light,
there can be no metaphor.

ALLAMA 972

CONCLUSION

In describing some of the general characteristics of Vīraśaivism through the vacanas, we have also described aspects of other bhakti-movements in India. The supreme importance of a guru, the celebration of a community of saints, worship as a personal relationship, the rejection of both great and little

22. *The Bhagavadgītā* XI, 12 'If in [bright] heaven together arise the shining brilliance of a thousand suns, then would that perhaps resemble the brilliance of that [God] so great of Self.' Tr. R. C. Zaehner, Oxford, 1969.

traditions (especially caste barriers), the wandering nature of the saint, the use of a common stock of religious ideas and symbols in the spoken language of the region, and the use of certain esoteric systems, these are only some of the shared characteristics. Such sharing actually makes for one more pan-Indian tradition, bhakti, with regional variations.

Both the classical (in Sanskrit and in the regional languages) and folk literature of India work with well-established languages of convention, given personae, and elaborate metrical patterns that mediate and depersonalize literary expression. The literary ideal is impersonality. But vacanas are personal literature, personal in several senses:

(a) Many of them express the real conflicts of real persons, represent a life more fully than anything in the older literature. For instance, Basavaṇṇa speaks of himself as the minister of of a non-Vīraśaiva king, accused by his own men of betraying his god for a king.

(b) They are uttered, not through a persona or mask, but directly in the person of the poet himself, in his native local dialect and idiom, using the tones and language of personal conversation or outcry.

(c) Even the few given conventional stances of bhakti are expressed in terms of deeply-felt personal relations; the loves and frustrations of bhakti are those of lover and beloved (e.g., Mahādēvi), mother and child, father and son, master and servant, even whore and customer.

(d) Compared to other Indian religious literatures like the Vedic hymns, the vacanas describe the devotee's state directly and the god only by implication; the concern is with the subject rather than the object (of worship).

Furthermore, bhakti religions like Vīraśaivism are Indian analogues to European protestant movements. Here we suggest a few parallels: protest against mediators like priest, ritual, temples, social hierarchy, in the name of direct, individual, original experience; a religious movement of and for the underdog, including saints of all castes and trades (like Bunyan, the tinker), speaking the sub-standard dialect of the region, producing often the first authentic regional expressions and translations of inaccessible Sanskritic texts (like the translations of the Bible in Europe); a religion of arbitrary grace, with a doctrine of the mystically chosen elect, replacing a social hierarchy-by-birth with a mystical hierarchy-by-experience; doctrines of work as worship leading to a puritan ethic; monotheism and evangelism, a mixture of intolerance and humanism, harsh and tender.

The vacanas express a kin-sense and kindness for all living things – not unknown to classical Hindu religion, but never so insistent and ardent – a love of man, beast and thing, asserting everywhere that man's arrangements are for man and not man for them. Basavaṇṇa cries out in one vacana (194):

They say: Pour, pour the milk!
  when they see a snake image in a stone.
But they cry: Kill, kill!
  when they meet a snake for real.

His most-quoted saying in Kannada asks, 'Where is religion without loving-kindness?' A poignant example of such loving-kindness towards all creation was the saint named Dasarēśwara. He did not even pick flowers to offer them to a god; he gathered only blossoms that fell of themselves:

Knowing one's lowliness
in every word;

the spray of insects in the air
in every gesture of the hand;

things living, things moving
come sprung from the earth
under every footfall;

and when holding a plant
or joining it to another
or in the letting it go

to be all mercy
to be light
as a dusting brush
of peacock feathers:

such moving, such awareness
is love that makes us one
with the Lord
Dasarēśwara.

DASARĒŚWARA

Further Readings in English

Bhandarkar, R. G., *Vaiṣṇavism, Śaivism, and Other Minor Religious Systems*. Strassburg, 1913.

Bhoosnurmath, S. S., and Menezes, L. M. A., *Śūnyasaṁpādane*, Vol. II (text and English translation). Dharwar, 1968; Vol. III, 1969.

Eliade, M., *Yoga: Immortality and Freedom*. New York, 1958.

Hastings, James, (ed.). *Encyclopaedia of Religion and Ethics*. New York, 1928. 13 volumes.

Especially: Enthoven, R. E., 'Lingayats', Vol. VIII.
Grierson, G. A., 'Bhakti-marga', Vol. II.

Lord, A. B., *The Singer of Tales*. Cambridge, Mass., 1960.

McCormack, W., 'The Forms of Communication in Vīraśaiva Religion', *Traditional India: Structure and Change*, ed. M. Singer, Philadelphia, 1957.

Nandimath, S. C., Menezes, L. M. A., and Hiremath, R. C. *Śūnyasaṁpādane* Vol. I (text and English translation). Dharwar: Karnatak University, 1965.

Nandimath, S. C., *A Handbook of Vīraśaivism*. Dharwar, 1942.

Raghavan, V., *The Great Integrators*. New Delhi, 1966.

Singer, M., *When a Great Tradition Modernizes*, an anthropological approach to Indian Civilization, New York, 1972.

Tipperudraswami, H., *The Vīraśaiva Saints*. Translated from the Kannada by S. M. Angadi. Mysore, 1968.

Turner, V., *The Ritual Process: Structure and Anti-Structure*. Chicago, 1969.

Weber, M., *The Religion of India*. Translated by Hans H. Gerth and Don Martindale. Glencoe, 1958.

Whitehead, H., *The Village Gods of South India*. Calcutta, 1921.

Zaehner, R. C., *The Bhagavadgītā*. Oxford, 1969.

SPEAKING OF ŚIVA

BASAVAṆṆA

THE biography of Basavaṇṇa has many contradictory sources: controversial edicts, deifying accounts by Vīraśaiva followers, poetic life-histories, pejorative accounts by his Jaina opponents mentioned in the vacanas of contemporary and later saints. Basavaṇṇa was a political activist and social reformer, minister to a king in a troubled century; it is not surprising that he should have been praised as a prophet by followers and condemned as a zealot and conspirator by his enemies, of whom he had many.

Leaving aside the scholarly and other controversies regarding the dates and the events of Basavaṇṇa's life, here is one generally accepted version:

Basavaṇṇa was born in A.D. 1106 and died in 1167 or 1168. His birthplace was probably Maṇigavaḷḷi. His parents seem to have died early in his childhood and he grew up under a grandmother's care; he was later looked after by his foster-parents, Mādirāja (or Mādarasa) and Mādāmbike of Bāgēvāḍi, who are often considered his own parents. His foster-father, Mādirāja, appears to have been learned in the traditional classics; Basavaṇṇa's Sanskrit learning obviously derives from his early education and environment. There are also records of a brahminical initiation ceremony (*upanayana*) in 1114 A.D. There is some reason to believe that Bijjaḷa, later Basavaṇṇa's patron and king, married the daughter of Mādirāja, and so was well-known to Basavaṇṇa even from his early years.

Basavaṇṇa had always been devoted to Śiva; by the time he was sixteen he decided to spend his life in the worship and service of Śiva. He found the caste-system of his society and the ritualism of his home shackling and senseless. As

Harihara, his fifteenth-century poet-biographer says, '"Love of Śiva cannot live with ritual." So saying, he tore off his sacred thread which bound him like a past-life's deeds . . . and left the shade of his home, disregarded wealth and propriety, thought nothing of relatives. Asking no one in town, he left Bāgēvāḍi, raging for the Lord's love, eastwards . . . and entered Kappaḍisaṅgama' where three rivers meet.

The Lord of the Meeting Rivers, *Kūḍalasaṅgamadēva*, becomes his chosen god; every vacana by Basavaṇṇa has his chosen god's name in it, usually as the closing signature-line.

In Kūḍalasaṅgama, he found a guru, with whom he studied the Vēdas and other religious texts. Though he began his worship with an external symbol (*sthāvaraliṅga*), he soon found his *iṣṭaliṅga*, his own personal, chosen, liṅga. Legend says that the Lord appeared to him in a dream and said, 'Son, Basavaṇṇa, we want to raise you in the world; go to Maṅgaḷavāḍa where King Bijjaḷa reigns.' Basavaṇṇa woke up and found it unbearable to follow the Lord's decree, leaving the temple and the Lord of the Meeting Rivers behind. He cried out that the Lord was merciless, 'taking away earth from under a man falling from the sky, cutting the throat of the faithful'. The Lord appeared to him again in a dream in the midst of his distress and said to him that he would appear next day to him through the mouth of the Sacred Bull. Next day while Basavaṇṇa waited worshipfully, leaning his body on the Stone Bull in the temple, the Lord formed a liṅga in the heart-lotus of the Bull, and enthroned on the tongue, came into Basavaṇṇa's hand, and initiated him. From then on, Basavaṇṇa was freed from places. He was his Lord's man and prepared himself to create a society of Śiva's men.

Basavaṇṇa then went to Kalyāṇa where his uncle Baladēva was Bijjaḷa's minister, and married his uncle's daughter

Gaṅgāmbike. Soon he was a trusted friend of King Bijjaḷa, and rose in his court. When his uncle Baladēva died, Basavaṇṇa succeeded him as Bijjaḷa's minister, and assumed many powers of state. He also gave his foster-sister, Nīlalōcane, to Basavaṇṇa in marriage.

Meanwhile, Basavaṇṇa's devotion matured from strength to strength. 'Not only was he the king's treasurer (*bhaṇḍāri*) but he became the Treasurer of the Lord's Love (*bhakti-bhaṇḍāri*)'. As the Lord and his jaṅgamas (wandering devotees) are both one, he fed and served the Lord's men. For 'they are the face and mouth of the Lord, as the root below is the mouth of a tree'. Devotees from far and near walked a beaten path to Kalyāṇa to see Basavaṇṇa and enjoy his hospitality. Many were converted to Śiva-worship by the fire of Basavaṇṇa's zeal and stayed in Kalyāṇa, thus swelling the numbers of Vīraśaivas. Basavaṇṇa also undertook the work of initiating the newcomers himself. A new community with egalitarian ideals disregarding caste, class and sex grew in Kalyāṇa, challenging orthodoxy, rejecting social convention and religious ritual. A political crisis was at hand.

Naturally, there was fierce opposition to this rising utopian ginger-group. Its enemies gathered around Bijjaḷa and battered at his faith in his minister with gossip and accusation. Bijjaḷa was swayed by this barrage of accusations and waited for a suitable opportunity to curb the rise of Vīraśaivism in his country.

In the new egalitarian Vīraśaiva community a wedding took place between two devotees; the bridegroom was a former outcaste and the bride an ex-brahmin. The traditionalists thought of this unorthodox marriage as the first blow against a society built on the caste-system. So Bijjaḷa sentenced the fathers of the bride and the bridegroom to death; they were dragged to death in the dust and thorn of the streets. The Vīraśaiva community, instead of being cowed by it, was roused to revenge and violence against 'state and society'. Basavaṇṇa, committed to non-violence, tried hard to convert the extremists but failed. In his failure, he left Kalyāṇa and returned to Kappaḍisaṅgama, where he died soon after (1166/1168?).

Meanwhile, extremist youths were out for revenge; they stabbed Bijjaḷa and assassinated him. In the riots and persecution that followed Vīraśaivas were scattered in all directions.

But in the brief period, probably the span of one generation, Basavaṇṇa had helped create a new community. Many great men like Allamaprabhu, saint of saints, were in Kalyāṇa in that period. He helped clear and shape the ideas of the Vīraśaivas. Many others like Siddharāma, Mācidēva, Bo:nmayya ('the lute-playing Bommayya'), and the remarkable radical woman-saint Mahādēviyakka were part of the company of saints. A religious centre called Anubhavamaṇṭapa ('the Hall of Experience') was established in which the great saints met for dialogue and communion, shaping the growing new community. A hundred and ninety thousand jaṅgamas or mendicant devotees are counted as having lived in Kalyāṇa under Basavaṇṇa's direction, helping spread the new religion.

Basavaṇṇa's achievement, in addition to the great vacanas he composed, was the establishment of a Vīraśaivism, with eight distinctive features,[1] based on a rejection of inequality of every kind, of ritualism and taboo, and exalting work (*kāyaka*) in the world in the name of the Lord.

Basavaṇṇa's vacanas have often been arranged according to an enlarged six-phase system (cf. appendix). For instance, Basavanāḷ, following no doubt earlier editors and commentators, divides the phases into several sub-phases; the rationale for such divisions is esoteric and technical. I shall

1. cf. footnote p. 32.

content myself here with an indication of the main six-phase classification, according to the editor:

Bhakta	1–527
Māhēśvara	528–765
Prasādi	766–795
Prāṇaliṅgi	796–918
Aikya	919–958

It is significant that though each saint goes through all the stages, he is most intensely expressive in some rather than in all equally. Further studies of this interesting typological framework and these expressive distributions in the saints' works will be rewarding. For instance, nearly half the vacanas of Basavaṇṇa are in the first phase of a man struggling with the world, its ills and temptations (compare Allama).

For the texts, the order and the numbering of the Basavaṇṇa vacanas I have used S. S. Basavanāḷ's edition (Dharwar, 1962).

8

Look, the world, in a swell
of waves, is beating upon my face.[1]*

Why should it rise to my heart,
tell me.
O tell me, why is it
rising now to my throat?
Lord,
how can I tell you anything
when it is risen high
over my head
lord lord
listen to my cries
O lord of the meeting rivers[2]
listen.

9

I added day by day
a digit[3] of light
like the moon.
The python-world,
omnivorous Rāhu,[4]
devoured me.

Today my body
is in eclipse.[5]
When is the release,
O lord of the meeting rivers?

* Notes to poems begin on p. 189.

21

Father, in my ignorance you brought me
through mothers' wombs,
through unlikely worlds.

Was it wrong just to be born,
  O lord?

Have mercy on me for being born
  once before.
    I give you my word,
    lord of the meeting rivers,
    never to be born again.

33

Like a monkey on a tree
it leaps from branch to branch:
  how can I believe or trust
  this burning thing, this heart?[6]
  It will not let me go
  to my Father,
  my lord of the meeting rivers.

36

Nine hounds unleashed
on a hare,
  the body's lusts
cry out:
  Let go!
    Let go!

Let go! Let go!
cry the lusts
of the mind.

Will my heart reach you,
O lord of the meeting rivers,

before the sensual bitches[7]
touch and overtake?

52

Like a cow fallen into a quagmire[8]
  I make mouths at this corner and that,

  no one to look for me
  or find me

  till my lord sees this beast
  and lifts him out by the horns.

59

Cripple me, father,
that I may not go here and there.
Blind me, father,
that I may not look at this and that.
Deafen me, father,
that I may not hear anything else.

Keep me
at your men's[9] feet
looking for nothing else,
O lord of the meeting rivers.[10]

62

Don't make me hear all day
'Whose man, whose man, whose man is this?'

Let me hear, 'This man is mine, mine,
this man is mine.'

O lord of the meeting rivers,
make me feel I'm a son
of the house.[11]

64

Śiva, you have no mercy.
Śiva, you have no heart.

Why why did you bring me to birth,
  wretch in this world,
  exile from the other?

Tell me, lord,
don't you have one more
little tree or plant
made just for me?

70*

As a mother runs
close behind her child
with his hand on a cobra
or a fire,

  the lord of the meeting rivers
  stays with me
  every step of the way
  and looks after me.

* This poem is taken from Basavanāḷ's appendix to the poems.

97

The master of the house, is he at home, or isn't he?
    Grass on the threshold,
    dirt in the house:
The master of the house, is he at home, or isn't he?

    Lies in the body,
    lust in the heart:
no, the master of the house is not at home,
  our Lord of the Meeting Rivers.

99

Does it matter how long
a rock soaks in the water:
will it ever grow soft?

Does it matter how long
I've spent in worship,
when the heart is fickle?

Futile as a ghost
I stand guard over hidden gold,[12]

O lord of the meeting rivers.

101

When a whore with a child
takes on a customer for money,

neither child nor lecher
will get enough of her.

She'll go pat the child once,
then go lie with the man once,

neither here nor there.
Love of money is relentless,

my lord of the meeting rivers.[13]

105

A snake-charmer and his noseless wife,[14]
snake in hand, walk carefully
trying to read omens
for a son's wedding,

but they meet head-on
a noseless woman
and her snake-charming husband,
and cry 'The omens are bad!'

His own wife has no nose;
there's a snake in his hand.
What shall I call such fools
who do not know themselves

and see only the others,

O lord
of the meeting
rivers!

III

I went to fornicate,
but all I got was counterfeit.

I went behind a ruined wall,
but scorpions stung me.

The watchman who heard my screams
just peeled off my clothes.

I went home in shame,
my husband raised weals on my back.

All the rest, O lord of the meeting rivers,
the king took for his fines.

125

See-saw watermills bow their heads.
So what?
Do they get to be devotees
to the Master?

The tongs join hands.
So what?
Can they be humble in service
to the Lord?

Parrots recite.
So what?
Can they read the Lord?

How can the slaves of the Bodiless God,[15]
Desire,
        know the way
        our Lord's Men move
        or the stance of their standing?

129

The sacrificial lamb brought for the festival
ate up the green leaf brought for the decorations.[16]

Not knowing a thing about the kill,
it wants only to fill its belly:
born that day, to die that day.

But tell me:
        did the killers survive,
        O lord of the meeting rivers?

132

You can make them talk
if the serpent
has stung
them.

You can make them talk
if they're struck
by an evil planet.[17]

But you can't make them talk
if they're struck dumb
by riches.

Yet when Poverty the magician
enters, they'll speak
at once,

O lord of the meeting rivers.

144

The crookedness of the serpent
is straight enough for the snake-hole.

The crookedness of the river
is straight enough for the sea.

And the crookedness of our Lord's men
is straight enough for our Lord!

161

Before
  the grey reaches the cheek,
  the wrinkle the rounded chin
  and the body becomes a cage of bones:

before
  with fallen teeth
  and bent back
  you are someone else's ward:

before
  you drop your hand to the knee
  and clutch a staff:

before
  age corrodes
  your form:

before
  death touches you:

    worship
    our lord
    of the meeting rivers!

162

Look at them,
busy, making an iron frame[18]
for a bubble on the water
to make it safe!

Worship the all-giving lord,
and live
without taking on trust
the body's firmness.

212

Don't you take on
this thing called bhakti:

like a saw
it cuts when it goes

and it cuts again
when it comes.

If you risk your hand
with a cobra in a pitcher[19]
will it let you
pass?

350*

a grindstone hung at the foot
a deadwood log at the neck

the one will not let me float
and the other will not let me sink

O time's true enemy
O lord of the meeting rivers

tide me over this life at sea[20]
and bring me to

* This poem is taken from Basavanāḷ's appendix.

420

The root is the mouth
of the tree: pour water there
at the bottom
and, look, it sprouts green
at the top.

The Lord's mouth is his moving men,
feed them. The Lord will give you all.

You'll go to hell,
if, knowing they are the Lord,
you treat them as men.[21]

430

Out of your eighty-four hundred thousand[22] faces
put on just one
and come test me, ask me.

If you don't come and ask me,
I'll swear by the names of your elders.

Come in any face and ask me;
I'll give,
my lord of the meeting rivers.

468

I drink the water we wash your feet with,[23]
I eat the food of worship,
and I say it's yours, everything,
goods, life, honour:
he's really the whore who takes every last bit
of her night's wages,

and will take no words
for payment,

he, my lord of the meeting rivers!

487

Feet will dance,
eyes will see,
tongue will sing,
and not find content.
What else, what else
shall I do?

I worship with my hands,
the heart is not content.
What else shall I do?

Listen, my lord,
it isn't enough.
I have it in me
to cleave thy belly
and enter thee

O lord of the meeting rivers!

494

I don't know anything like time-beats and metre
nor the arithmetic of strings and drums;
I don't know the count of iamb and dactyl.[24]

My lord of the meeting rivers,
as nothing will hurt you
I'll sing as I love.

500

Make of my body the beam of a lute
  of my head the sounding gourd
  of my nerves the strings
  of my fingers the plucking rods.

Clutch me close
  and play your thirty-two songs
  O lord of the meeting rivers!

555

Certain gods[25]
always stand watch
at the doors of people.
Some will not go if you ask them to go.
Worse than dogs, some others.
What can they give,
these gods,
who live off the charity of people

  O lord of the meeting rivers?

558

How can I feel right
  about a god who eats up lacquer and melts,
  who wilts when he sees fire?[26]

How can I feel right
  about gods you sell in your need,
  and gods you bury for fear of thieves?

The lord of the meeting rivers,
self-born, one with himself,

he alone is the true god.

563

The pot is a god. The winnowing
fan is a god. The stone in the
street is a god. The comb is a
god. The bowstring is also a
god. The bushel is a god and the
spouted cup is a god.

Gods, gods, there are so many
there's no place left
for a foot.

There is only
one god. He is our Lord
of the Meeting Rivers.

581

They plunge
wherever they see water.

They circumambulate
every tree they see.

How can they know you
O Lord
who adore
waters that run dry
trees that wither?

586

In a brahmin house
where they feed the fire[27]
as a god

when the fire goes wild
and burns the house

they splash on it
the water of the gutter
and the dust of the street,

beat their breasts
and call the crowd.

These men then forget their worship
and scold their fire,
O lord of the meeting rivers!

639

You went riding elephants.
You went riding horses.
You covered yourself
with vermilion and musk.
                                        O brother,
but you went without the truth,
you went without sowing and reaping
the good.
                Riding rutting elephants
of pride, you turned easy target
to fate.
            You went without knowing
our lord of the meeting rivers.

You qualified for hell.

686

He'll grind till you're fine and small.
He'll file till your colour shows.

  If your grain grows fine
  in the grinding,
  if you show colour
  in the filing,

then our lord of the meeting rivers
will love you
and look after you.

703

Look here, dear fellow:
I wear these men's clothes
only for you.[28]

Sometimes I am man,
sometimes I am woman.

O lord of the meeting rivers
I'll make wars for you
but I'll be your devotees' bride.

705

If a rich son is born
to one born penniless,
he'll delight his father's heart
with gold counted in millions;

if a warrior son is born
to a milk-livered king
who doesn't know which way
to face a battle, he'll console
his father with a battlefront
sinking and floating
in a little sea of blood;

so will I console you
O lord of the meeting rivers,
if you should come
and ask me.

820

The rich[29]
will make temples for Śiva.
What shall I,
a poor man,
do?

My legs are pillars,
the body the shrine,
the head a cupola[30]
of gold.

Listen, O lord of the meeting rivers,
things standing[31] shall fall,
but the moving[32] ever shall stay.

831

I'm no worshipper;
I'm no giver;
I'm not even beggar,

O lord
without your grace.

Do it all yourself, my lord of meeting rivers,
as a mistress would
when maids are sick.[33]

847

When
like a hailstone crystal
like a waxwork image
the flesh melts in pleasure
   how can I tell you?

The waters of joy
broke the banks
and ran out of my eyes.

I touched and joined
my lord of the meeting rivers.
How can I talk to anyone
of that?

848

Sir, isn't the mind witness enough,
   for the taste on the tongue?

Do buds wait for the garland maker's word
   to break into flower?

Is it right, sir, to bring out the texts
   for everything?

And, sir, is it really right to bring into the open
   the mark on our vitals
   left by our lord's love-play?

860

The eating bowl is not one bronze
and the looking glass another.

Bowl and mirror are one metal.
Giving back light
one becomes a mirror.

Aware, one is the Lord's;
unaware, a mere human.

Worship the lord without forgetting,
the lord of the meeting rivers.

885

Milk is left over
from the calves.
Water is left over
from the fishes,
flowers from the bees.

How can I worship you,
O Śiva, with such offal?
But it's not for me
to despise left-overs,
so take what comes,

lord of the meeting rivers.

DĒVARA DĀSIMAYYA

DĒVARA DĀSIMAYYA or 'God's Dāsimayya' was probably the earliest of the vacana poets. Commentators, and later saints like Basavaṇṇa, make admiring references to him in their writings.

He is said to have been born in Mudanūru, a village full of temples, in the tenth century. His village has a Rāmanātha temple among its many temples, dedicated to Śiva as worshipped by Rāma, the epic hero, an incarnation of Viṣṇu. Every vacana of Dāsimayya is addressed to Rāmanātha, 'Rāma's lord'.

Legend says that he performed ascetic penance in a dense forest when Śiva appeared to him, advised him not to punish his body to follow the way of the liṅga, the all-encompassing symbol. The Lord taught him that working in the world (*kāyaka*) was a part of worshipping and reaching Him. Dāsimayya became a weaver. So he is also known as Jēḍara Dāsimayya or 'Dāsimayya of the weavers'.

Today in Mudanūru, popular tradition identifies several places where Dāsimayya set up his weaver's looms.

Many stories are told about Dāsimayya's achievements as a propagator of Vīraśaiva religion. Once he met jungle tribes who hunted wild animals and lived on their flesh. He converted them to the non-violent ways of liṅga worship and taught them the use of the oil-press for their living. Another time, he was challenged by brahmins. They said to him: 'Your Śiva is the chieftain of demons; he covers his body with ash. Give him up. Worship our Viṣṇu and find a place for yourself.' He answered: 'Your Viṣṇu in his incarnations has come through the womb of a pig; and stolen butter from villagers. Was that right and proper?' In the course of the argument he said that Śiva was everywhere. The brahmins challenged him to show Śiva in their Viṣṇu temple. Dāsimayya accepted the challenge, and invoked Śiva. When they all entered the temple, the image in the shrine was not that of Viṣṇu but a liṅga. The brahmins, struck by the miracle, were all converted.[1]

When he decided to marry, he found suitable a girl named Duggaḷe. He went to her parents in the village of Śivapura. Showing them some sand, he said he would marry their daughter if she could boil it into edible rice.[2] Duggaḷe, a devotee, washed the saint's feet, sprinkled the sand with some of the washings and cooked it. The sand became rice. Dāsimayya, convinced that Duggaḷe was a true devotee, married her.

Once he started weaving on his loom an enormous turban-cloth in the Lord's name. It was a marvel of workmanship. When he took it to the fair to sell it, no buyer could price such beauty. When a thief in the crowd tried to steal it, a sharp wheel whirled out of it and slashed his hand. The people thought that the cloth was holy and magical and would not buy it. On his way back home he was met by an old man. The old man was shivering in the cold and asked him for the cloth. Dāsimayya gave it to him at once. The old man laughed, tore up the precious piece to bits right before his eyes, wrapped one strip on his head, another round his body, still another on his hand; the rest he swathed round his staff. Dāsimayya looked on and said calmly: 'It is yours. You can use it as you wish.' He brought the eccentric old

1. This legend, taken with poems regarding the supremacy of Śiva over all other gods (e.g. 4), speaks of the struggle of Vīraśaivism in the saint's times. 'Vīraśaivism' means 'militant or heroic Śaivism'. Dāsimayya's signature Rāmanātha, 'Lord of Rāma', is also significantly chosen to assert Śiva's primacy.

2. A common marriage-test for brides in Indian folklore – somewhat like spinning straw into gold in the Rumpelstiltskin tale.

man home, fed him and served him in all possible ways. The old man was Śiva himself. Pleased with Dāsimayya and his wife, and their way of life, and filled with compassion for their hardship and poverty, Śiva gave Duggaḷe a handful of rice. He asked her to mix it with the rest of her store. The divine rice made her store inexhaustible (*akṣaya*) and self-renewing.

Dāsimayya became a famous teacher in the kingdom of Jayasiṁha the Cālukya king. The king was a *jaina*. But Suggale, his queen, came from a Śaivite family and received initiation from Dāsimayya. The king and his jaina followers were outraged by this act and planned to defeat the saint in argument. Once they hid a boy in the bole of a tree and told Dāsimayya that their omnipresent god was also in the tree. In demonstration, they called out to the tree. But no answer came as expected. When they looked into the tree, the boy was dead. The boy's mother cried and begged of Dāsimayya to give him life, which he did. His enemies also tested him by asking him to drink of a filthy poisoned tank; by the help of Śiva, Dāsimayya drew away all the filth and poison and drank the water without harm. Dāsimayya's body, inviolate, foiled all assassins. Finally his enemies went to the king, complained to him about all the jaina temples that had become rededicated to Śiva since the queen's initiation. The king had an argument with his queen, who was living apart. She told him that Śiva was the true god and challenged all the anti-Śaivites to an argument with Dāsimayya. A day was set. Pundits of every cult and colour joined the religious battle in the king's court. Dāsimayya's arguments were unanswerable and silenced all opponents. Yet the jainas, thinking evil in their hearts, brought a deadly serpent hidden in a pitcher and asked Dāsimayya to show his god in it. When he took off the lid, the serpent spread out its hood and hissed venomously. The saint said, 'Śiva is the only god,' and held the reptile in his hand. At once it turned into a crystal liṅga which he set down, establishing a temple on the spot. The king was converted; he and all his family received initiation from Dāsimayya. The 700 jaina temples were converted into liṅga temples, and the 20,000 citizens of the city became Śaivites.

Dāsimayya returned to Mudanūru and resumed his weaving. When he wished to give up the world and enter god, he went to the Rāmanātha temple and told Rāmanātha: 'I've lived my life and done everything by your grace. Now you must return me to yourself.' Rāmanātha was pleased and appeared to him in his true form. Dāsimayya's wife Duggaḷe said to the Lord: 'My husband's path is mine. With him you must take me too.' So he and Duggaḷe praised the Lord together and entered the infinite.

All these legends speak eloquently of Dāsimayya, the missionary for Vīraśaivism, and the way he converted men of all sorts, jungle tribes, brahmins and jaina kings, to his religion. They also speak of the early conflicts of Vīraśaivism with all the contemporary religions. Śri Śaila, the centre for Vīraśaiva saints, seems to have become such a centre as early as the tenth century, the time of the earliest vacana saint, Dāsimayya. His vacanas do mention earlier saints and their vacanas but his and others' references are all we have for evidence.

We are indebted to Rao Bahadūr Pha. Gu. Haḷakaṭṭi's (Bijapur) 1955 edition for the vacana texts and the above legends. The order and numbering of the vacanas follow his arrangement.

The first twenty-one vacanas of Dāsimayya deal with a variety of themes like the nature of god (e.g. 4), salvation, etc. The rest are arranged by the editor according to the six-phase system (cf. Appendix I):

Bhakta phase	23–87
Māhēśvara	88–98
Prasādi	99–113
Prāṇaliṅgi	114–124
Śaraṇa	125–141
Aikya	142–147

4

You balanced the globe
on the waters
and kept it from melting away,[34]

you made the sky stand
without pillar or prop.

O Rāmanātha,
which gods could have
done this?

23

In the mother's womb
the child does not know
his mother's face

nor can *she* ever know
his face.

The man in the world's illusion
does not know the Lord

nor the Lord him,

Rāmanātha.

24

If this is my body
would it not follow my will?

If this is your body
would it not follow your will?

Obviously, it is neither your body
nor mine:
it is the fickle body
of the burning world you made,

Rāmanātha.

25

Hunger the great serpent
has seized the vitals
and the venom is mounting
from foot to brow.

Only he is the true Snake-man
in all the world
who can feed this hunger food

and bring the poison down,

Rāmanātha.[35]

26

A fire
in every act and look and word.
Between man and wife
a fire.
In the plate of food
eaten after much waiting
a fire.
In the loss of gain
a fire.
And in the infatuation
of coupling
a fire.

You have given us
five fires
and poured dirt in our mouths

O Rāmanātha.

42

A man filled grain
in a tattered sack
and walked all night
fearing the toll-gates

but the grain went through the tatters
and all he got was the gunny sack.

It is thus
with the devotion
of the faint-hearted

O Rāmanātha.

43

Can assemblies in session
give charities to men?

Everyone who goes to war
goes only to die.

Only one in a hundred,
may be one in a thousand,

gets to spear the enemy.

O Rāmanātha
how can every tamarind flower
be fruit?[36]

44

For what
shall I handle a dagger
O lord?

What can I pull it out of,
or stab it in,

when You are all the world,

O Rāmanātha?

45

The five elements
have become one.

The sun and the moon,
O Rider of the Bull,[37]
aren't they really
your body?

I stand,
look on,
you're filled
with the worlds.

What can I hurt now
after this, Rāmanātha?

49

For your devotees
I shall be
bullock; for your devotees
I shall be
menial,
slave and watchdog
at the door:

Maker of all things, for men
who raise their hands
in your worship

I shall be the fence of thorns
on their backyard

O Rāmanātha.

55

When a man is of the Lord
and his wife, of the world,
what they eat is still
shared equally:

it is like
bringing a dead dog
into the attic
and sharing bits
of its carcass,

O Rāmanātha.[38]

72

You have forged
this chain
of eighteen links[39]
and chained us humans:

you have ruined us
O Rāmanātha
and made us dogs forever
on the leash.

80

The earth is your gift,
the growing grain your gift,
the blowing wind your gift.

What shall I call these curs
who eat out of your hand
and praise everyone else?

87

Whatever It was

that made this earth
the base,
the world its life,
the wind its pillar,
arranged the lotus and the moon,
and covered it all with folds
of sky

with Itself inside,

to that Mystery
indifferent to differences,

to It I pray,
O Rāmanātha.

90

He will make them roam the streets;
scrape them on stone for colour of gold;
grind them for sandal;
like a stick of sugarcane
he will slash them to look inside.

If they do not wince or shudder,
he will pick them up by the hands,

will our Rāmanātha.

94

What does it matter
if the fox roams
all over the Jambu island?
Will he ever stand amazed
in meditation of the Lord?
Does it matter if he wanders
all over the globe
and bathes in a million sacred rivers?[40]

A pilgrim who's not one with you,
Rāmanātha,
roams the world
like a circus man.

96

Did the breath of the mistress
have breasts and long hair?

Or did the master's breath
wear sacred thread?

Did the outcaste, last in line,
hold with his outgoing breath
the stick of his tribe?

What do the fools of this world know
of the snares you set,
O Rāmanātha?

98

To the utterly at-one with Śiva

there's no dawn,
no new moon,
no noonday,
nor equinoxes,
nor sunsets,
nor full moons;

his front yard
is the true Benares,

O Rāmanātha.

120

I'm the one who has the body,
you're the one who holds the breath.

You know the secret of my body,
I know the secret of your breath.

That's why your body
is in mine.

You know
and I know, Rāmanātha,

the miracle

of your breath
in my body.

121

God of my clan,
I'll not place my feet
but where your feet
have stood before:
I've no feet
of my own.

How can the immoralists
of this world know
the miracle, the oneness
of your feet
and mine,

Rāmanātha?

123

Bodied,
one will hunger.

Bodied,
one will lie.

O you, don't you rib
and taunt me
again
for having a body:

body Thyself for once
like me and see
what happens,

O Rāmanātha.

124

When, to the hungerless figure,
you serve waters of no thirst,
whisper the sense-less word
in the heart,
and call without a name,

who is it that echoes O!
in answer,
O Rāmanātha,

is it you,
or is it me?

126

Unless you build,
Space will not get inside
a house;

unless the eye sees,
mind will not decide
on forms;

without a way
there's no reaching
the other;

O Rāmanātha
how will men know
that this is so?

127

Fire can burn
but cannot move.

Wind can move
but cannot burn.

Till fire joins wind
it cannot take a step.

Do men know
it's like that
with knowing and doing?

128

Can the wind bring out
and publish for others
the fragrance
in the little bud?

Can even begetters, father and mother,
display for onlookers' eyes
the future breast and flowing hair
in the little girl
about to be bride?

Only ripeness
can show consequence,

Rāmanātha.

131

Rāmanātha,
who can know the beauty
of the Hovering One

who's made Himself form
and of space
the colours?

133

If they see
breasts and long hair coming
they call it woman,

if beard and whiskers
they call it man:

but, look, the self that hovers
in between
is neither man
nor woman

O Rāmanātha

144

Suppose you cut a tall bamboo
in two;
make the bottom piece a woman,
the headpiece a man;
rub them together
till they kindle:
tell me now,
the fire that's born,
is it male or female,

O Rāmanātha?

MAHĀDĒVIYAKKA

MAHĀDĒVI, a younger contemporary of Basavaṇṇa and Allama in the twelfth century, was born in Uḍutaḍi, a village in Śivamogga, near the birthplace of Allama. At ten, she was initiated to Śiva-worship by an unknown guru. She considered that moment the moment of her real birth. Apparently, the form of Śiva at the Uḍutaḍi temple was Mallikārjuna, translated either as 'the Lord White as Jasmine' or as 'Arjuna, Lord of goddess Mallikā'. 'Cenna' means 'lovely, beautiful'. She fell in love with Cennamallikārjuna and took his name for a 'signature' (*aṅkita*) in all her vacanas.

She betrothed herself to Śiva and none other, but human lovers pressed their suit. The rivalry between the Divine Lover and all human loves was dramatized by the incidents of her own life (vacana 114). Kauśika, the king (or chieftain) of the land, saw her one day and fell in love with her. He sent word to her parents, asking for her hand. In addition to being only human, he disqualified himself further by being a *bhavi*, an unbeliever. Yet he persuaded her, or rather her parents, partly by show of force, and partly by his protestations of love. It is quite likely that she married him and lived with him, though some scholars dispute the tainting fact. Anyhow it must have been a trying marriage for both. Kauśika, the wordling, full of desire for her as a mortal, was the archetype of sensual man; Mahādēvi, a spirit married already to the Lord White as Jasmine, scorning all human carnal love as corrupt and illegitimate, wife to no man, exile bound to the world's wheeling lives, archetypal sister of all souls. Significantly she is known as Akka 'elder sister'. Many of Mahādēvi's most moving vacanas speak of this conflict (cf. 114). Sometimes, the Lord is her illicit lover (cf. 88), sometimes her only legitimate husband (cf. 283). This ambiguous alternation of attitudes regarding the legitimacy of living in the world is a fascinating aspect of Mahādēvi's poetry.

At one point, Kauśika appears to have tried to force his will on her and so she leaves him, cutting clean her relations with the whole world of men. Like many another saint, enacting his true homelessness by his wanderings, she left birthplace and parents (102). She appears to have thrown away even modesty and clothing, those last concessions to the male world, in a gesture of ultimate social defiance, and wandered about covered in her tresses (124).

Through a world of molesting male attentions she wandered, defiant and weary (294), asserting the legitimacy of her illicit love for the Lord, searching for him and his devotees. She walked towards Kalyāṇa, the centre of Vīraśaiva saints, the 'halls of Experience' where Allama and Basavaṇṇa ran a school for kindred spirits.

Allama did not accept her at once. A remarkable conversation ensued, a dialogue between sceptic and love-child which turned into a catechism between guru and disciple. Many of Mahādēvi's vacanas are placed by legend in this famous dialogue.[1] When Allama asked the wild-looking woman for her husband's identity, she replied she was married forever to Cennamallikārjuna. He asked her then the obvious question: 'Why take off clothes, as if by that gesture you could peel off illusions? And yet robe yourself in tresses of hair? If so free and pure in heart, why replace a sari with a covering of tresses?' Her reply is honest:

> Till the fruit is ripe inside
> the skin will not fall off.

1. Recorded or reconstructed in *Śūnyasampādane* (ca. fifteenth century) cf. note on Allama Prabhu, p. 144.

I'd a feeling it would hurt you
if I displayed the body's seals of love.
O brother, don't tease me
needlessly. I'm given entire
into the hands of my lord
white as jasmine.

MAHĀDĒVIYAKKA 183

For other such contexts, see also vacanas 104, 157, 184, 251, 283, and the notes on them.

At the end of this ordeal by dialogue she was accepted into the company of saints. From then begins the second lap of her journey to her Lord. She wandered wild and god-intoxicated, in love with him, yet not finding him. Restless, she left Kalyāṇa and wandered off again towards Śrīśaila, the Holy Mountain, where she found him and lost herself. Her search is recorded in her vacanas as a search for her love, following all the phases of human love as set forth by the conventions of Indian, especially Sanskrit, poetry. The three chief forms of love, love forbidden (e.g., 328), love in separation (e.g., 318) and love in union (e.g., 336) are all expressed in her poems, often one attitude informing and complicating another in the same poem (e.g., 318).

She was recognized by her fellow-saints as the most poetic of them all, with a single symbolic action unifying all her poetry. She enlists the traditional imagery of pan-Indian secular love-poetry for personal expression. In her, the phases of human love are metaphors for the phases of mystic ascent. In this search, unlike the other saints, she involves all of nature, a sister to bird, beast and tree (e.g., 73). Appropriately, she chose for adoration an aesthetic aspect of Śiva, Śiva as Cennamallikārjuna, or the Lovely Lord White as Jasmine.

Like other bhaktas, her struggle was with her condition, as body, as woman, as social being tyrannized by social roles, as a human confined to a place and a time. Through these shackles she bursts, defiant in her quest for ecstasy.

According to legend, she died into 'oneness with Śiva' when she was hardly in her twenties – a brief bright burning.

I have used L. Basavarāju's edition of Mahādēviyakka's vacanas: *Akkana Vacanagaḷu* (Mysore, 1966). The numbers follow Basavarāju's edition, which does not classify her vacanas according to the six-phase system.

2

Like
treasure hidden in the ground
taste in the fruit
gold in the rock
oil in the seed

the Absolute hidden away
in the heart

no one can know
the ways of our lord

white as jasmine.[41]

11

You're like milk
in water:[42] I cannot tell
what comes before,
what after;
which is the master,
which the slave;
what's big,
what's small.

O lord white as jasmine
if an ant should love you
and praise you,
will he not grow
to demon powers?

12

My body is dirt,[43]
my spirit is space:
which
shall I grab, O lord? How,
and what,
shall I think of you?
Cut through
my illusions,
lord white as jasmine.

17

Like a silkworm[44] weaving
her house with love
from her marrow,
and dying
in her body's threads
winding tight, round
and round,
I burn
desiring what the heart desires.

Cut through, O lord,
my heart's greed,
and show me
your way out,

O lord white as jasmine.

18

Not one, not two, not three or four,
but through eighty-four hundred thousand[45] vaginas
have I come,
I have come
through unlikely worlds,
guzzled on
pleasure and on pain.
Whatever be
all previous lives,
show me mercy
this one day,
O lord
white as jasmine.

20

Monkey on monkeyman's stick
puppet at the end of a string

I've played as you've played
I've spoken as you've told me
I've been as you've let me be

O engineer of the world
lord white as jasmine

I've run
till you cried halt.

26

Illusion has troubled body as shadow
troubled life as a heart
troubled heart as a memory
troubled memory as awareness.

With stick raised high, Illusion herds
the worlds.
Lord white as jasmine
no one can overcome
your Illusion.

45

It was like a stream
running into the dry bed
of a lake,
like rain
pouring on plants
parched to sticks.

It was like this world's pleasure
and the way to the other,
both
walking towards me.

Seeing the feet of the master,
O lord white as jasmine,
I was made
worthwhile.

50

When I didn't know myself
where were you?

Like the colour in the gold,
you were in me.

I saw in you,
lord white as jasmine,
the paradox of your being
in me
without showing a limb.

60

Not seeing you
in the hill, in the forest,
from tree to tree[46]
I roamed,
searching, gasping:
Lord, my Lord, come
show me your kindness!

till I met your men
and found you.
You hide
lest I seek and find.
Give me a clue,
O lord
white as jasmine,
to your hiding places.

65

If sparks fly
I shall think my thirst and hunger quelled.

If the skies tear down
I shall think them pouring for my bath.

If a hillside slide on me
I shall think it flower for my hair.

O lord white as jasmine, if my head falls from my shoulders
I shall think it your offering.

68

Locks of shining red hair
a crown of diamonds[47]
small beautiful teeth
and eyes in a laughing face
that light up fourteen worlds –
  I saw His glory,
and seeing, I quell today
the famine in my eyes.

I saw the haughty Master
for whom men, all men,
are but women, wives.

I saw the Great One
who plays at love
with Śakti,
original to the world,

I saw His stance
and began to live.

69

O mother[48] I burned
in a flameless fire

O mother I suffered
a bloodless wound

mother I tossed
without a pleasure:

loving my lord white as jasmine
I wandered through unlikely worlds.

73

O twittering birds,
don't you know? don't you know?

O swans on the lakeshore,
don't you know? don't you know?

O high-singing koils,[49]
don't you know? don't you know?

O circling swooping bees,
don't you know? don't you know?

O peacocks in the caverns,
don't you know?
don't you know?

Tell me if you know:
where is He,

my lord
white as jasmine?

74

O swarm of bees
O mango tree
O moonlight
O koilbird
I beg of you all
one
favour:

If you should see my lord anywhere
my lord white as jasmine

call out
and show him to me.

75

You are the forest

you are all the great trees
in the forest

you are bird and beast
playing in and out
of all the trees

O lord white as jasmine
filling and filled by all

why don't you
show me your face?

77

Would a circling surface vulture
  know such depths of sky
  as the moon would know?

would a weed on the riverbank
  know such depths of water
  as the lotus would know?

would a fly darting nearby
  know the smell of flowers
  as the bee would know?

O lord white as jasmine
  only you would know
  the way of your devotees:
  how would these,

these
  mosquitoes
  on the buffalo's hide?

79

Four parts of the day[50]
I grieve for you.
Four parts of the night
I'm mad for you.

I lie lost
sick for you, night and day,
O lord white as jasmine.

Since your love
was planted,
I've forgotten hunger,
thirst, and sleep.

87

Listen, sister, listen.
I had a dream

I saw rice, betel, palmleaf
and coconut.
I saw an ascetic[51]
come to beg,
white teeth and small matted curls.

I followed on his heels
and held his hand,
he who goes breaking
all bounds and beyond.

I saw the lord, white as jasmine,
and woke wide open.

88

He bartered my heart,
  looted my flesh,
  claimed as tribute
  my pleasure,
  took over
  all of me.

I'm the woman of love
for my lord, white as jasmine.

93

Other men are thorn
under the smooth leaf.
I cannot touch them,
go near them, nor trust them,
nor speak to them confidences.

Mother,[52]
because they all have thorns
in their chests,
                I cannot take
any man in my arms but my lord

  white as jasmine.

102

When one heart touches
  and feels another
won't feeling weigh over all,
can it stand any decencies then?

O mother,[53] you must be crazy,
I fell for my lord
  white as jasmine,
I've given in utterly.

Go, go, I'll have nothing
of your mother-and-daughter stuff.
You go now.

104

Till you've earned
knowledge of good and evil

  it is
  lust's body,
  site of rage,
  ambush of greed,
  house of passion,
  fence of pride,
  mask of envy.

Till you know and lose this knowing
you've no way
of knowing
my lord white as jasmine.[54]

114

Husband inside,
lover outside.
I can't manage them both.

This world
and that other,
cannot manage them both.

O lord white as jasmine

I cannot hold in one hand
both the round nut[55]
and the long bow.

117

Who cares
who strips a tree of leaf
once the fruit is plucked?

Who cares
who lies with the woman
you have left?

Who cares
who ploughs the land
you have abandoned?

After this body has known my lord
who cares if it feeds
a dog
or soaks up water?

119

What's to come tomorrow
let it come today.
What's to come today
let it come right now.

Lord white as jasmine,
don't give us your *nows* and *thens*!

120

Breath for fragrance,
who needs flowers?

with peace, patience, forgiving and self-command,
who needs the Ultimate Posture?

The whole world become oneself
who needs solitude,

O lord white as jasmine.[56]

124

You can confiscate
money in hand;
can you confiscate
the body's glory?

Or peel away every strip
you wear,
but can you peel
the Nothing, the Nakedness
that covers and veils?[57]

To the shameless girl
wearing the White Jasmine Lord's
light of morning,
you fool,
where's the need for cover and jewel?

131

Sunlight made visible
the whole length of a sky,
movement of wind,
leaf, flower, all six colours[58]
on tree, bush and creeper:
all this
is the day's worship.

The light of moon, star and fire,
lightnings and all things
that go by the name of light
are the night's worship.

Night and day
in your worship
I forget myself

O lord white as jasmine.

157

If one could
draw the fangs of a snake
and charm the snake to play,
it's great to have snakes.

If one can single out
the body's ways
it's great to have bodies.
The body's wrong
is like mother turning vampire.

Don't say they have bodies
who have Your love,
O lord
white as jasmine.[59]

184

People,
male and female,
blush when a cloth covering their shame
comes loose.
When the lord of lives
lives drowned without a face
in the world, how can you be modest?

When all the world is the eye of the lord,
onlooking everywhere, what can you
cover and conceal?

199

For hunger,
  there is the town's rice in the begging bowl.

For thirst,
  there are tanks, streams, wells.

For sleep,
  there are the ruins of temples.[60]

For soul's company
  I have you, O lord
white as jasmine.

200

Make me go from house to house
  with arms stretched for alms.

If I beg, make them give nothing.

If they give, make it fall to the ground.

If it falls, before I pick it up, make a dog take it,

O lord
white as jasmine.

251

Why do I need this dummy
  of a dying world?
  illusion's chamberpot,
  hasty passions' whorehouse,
  this crackpot
  and leaky basement?

Finger may squeeze the fig
  to feel it, yet not choose
  to eat it.

Take me, flaws and all,
O lord

white as jasmine.

274

Every tree
in the forest was the All-Giving Tree,
every bush
the life-reviving herb,
every stone the Philosophers' Stone,
all the land a pilgrim's holy place,
all the water nectar against age,
every beast the golden deer,
every pebble I stumble on
the Wishing Crystal:
  walking round
the Jasmine Lord's favourite hill,

  I happened
on the Plantain Grove.[61]

283

I love the Handsome One:
he has no death
decay nor form
no place or side
no end nor birthmarks.
I love him O mother. Listen.

I love the Beautiful One
with no bond nor fear
no clan no land
no landmarks
for his beauty.

So my lord, white as jasmine, is my husband.

Take these husbands who die,
decay, and feed them
to your kitchen fires!

294

O brothers,[62] why do you talk
to this woman,
hair loose,
face withered,
body shrunk?

O fathers, why do you bother
with this woman?
She has no strength of limb,
has lost the world,
lost power of will,
turned devotee,

she has lain down
with the Lord, white as jasmine,
and has lost caste.

313

Like an elephant
lost from his herd
suddenly captured,

remembering his mountains,
    his Vindhyas,
        I remember.

A parrot
come into a cage
remembering his mate,
        I remember.

O lord white as jasmine
show me
your ways.
    Call me: Child, come here,
        come this way.

317

Riding the blue sapphire mountains
wearing moonstone for slippers
blowing long horns
O Śiva
when shall I
crush you on my pitcher breasts

O lord white as jasmine
when do I join you
stripped of body's shame
and heart's modesty?

318

If He says
He has to go away
to fight battles at the front[63]
  I understand and can be quiet.

But how can I bear it
when He is here in my hands
right here in my heart
  and will not take me?

O mind, O memory of pasts,
if you will not help me get to Him
how can I ever bear it?

319

What do
the barren know
of birthpangs?

Stepmothers,
what do they know
of loving care?

How can the unwounded
know the pain
of the wounded?

O lord white as jasmine
your love's blade stabbed
and broken in my flesh,

I writhe.
O mothers
how can you know me?

321

The heart in misery
has turned
upside down.

The blowing gentle breeze
is on fire.[64]
O friend moonlight burns
like the sun.

Like a tax-collector in a town
I go restlessly here and there.

Dear girl go tell Him
bring Him to His senses.
Bring Him back.

My lord white as jasmine
is angry
that we are two.

322

My husband comes home today.
Wear your best, wear your jewels.

The Lord, white as jasmine,
will come anytime now.

Girls, come
meet Him at the door.

323

I look at the road
for his coming.
If he isn't coming,
I pine and waste away.
If he is late,
I grow lean.

O mother, if he is away
for a night,
I'm like the lovebird[65]
with nothing
in her embrace.

324

Better than meeting
and mating all the time
is the pleasure of mating once
after being far apart.

When he's away
I cannot wait
to get a glimpse of him.

Friend, when will I have it
both ways,
be with Him
yet not with Him,
my lord white as jasmine?

328

I have Māyā for mother-in-law;
  the world for father-in-law;
  three brothers-in-law, like tigers;

  and the husband's thoughts
  are full of laughing women:
    no god, this man.

And I cannot cross the sister-in-law.

But I will
give this wench the slip
and go cuckold my husband with Hara, my Lord.

  My mind is my maid:
  by her kindness, I join
  my Lord,
    my utterly beautiful Lord
    from the mountain-peaks,
    my lord white as jasmine,
and I will make Him
my good husband.

336

Look at
love's marvellous
ways:

if you shoot an arrow
plant it
till no feather shows;

if you hug
a body, bones
must crunch and crumble;

weld,
the welding must vanish.

Love is then
our lord's love.

ALLAMA PRABHU

THERE are two traditions regarding Allama's life. One considers him Śiva himself, arriving in the world to teach the way of freedom. To try him, Śiva's consort, Pārvati, sent down her dark side, Māye or Illusion. Allama's parents are named allegorically 'Selflessness' (*nirahaṅkāra*) and 'The Wise One' (*sujñāni*). Māye was born to parents named 'Selfishness' (*mamakāra*) and 'Lady Illusion' (*māyādēvi*). In this version, Allama was not even born: his parents undertook penance for their 'truth-bringing sorrowless' son, and found by their side a shining child. Thus, unborn, he descended into the world. Later, when he was playing the drum in a temple, Māye fell in love with him, and appointed him her dancing master. She tried all her charms on him but could not move him. Pārvati, who had sent him the temptation, realized that tempting him was useless and withdrew Māye to herself. A more human variant of this Descent-version speaks of Allama and the enchantress as minions of Śiva and Pārvati, cursed to be born in the world.

There are differences from variant to variant in the names of the parents, the place, and manner of birth. The most vivid tradition of this kind is the earliest, written up by Harihara, a brilliant fifteenth-century poet who wrote the lives of the Vīraśaiva saints in galloping blank verse. According to Harihara: Allama, talented temple-drummer, son of a dance teacher, falls in love with Kāmalate ('love's tendril'). In marriage, they were new lovers; their love was without 'end, beginning, or middle'; 'drowned in desire' knowing no weight or impediment. But Kāmalate was suddenly stricken down by a fever and died soon after. Allama wanders in his grief like a madman, benumbed, his memory eclipsed, his heart broken, calling out for the dead Kāmalate, in field, forest, village. While he was sitting in an out-of-town grove, downcast, scratching the ground idly with his toenail, he saw something: the golden kalaśa (pinnacle, cupola) of a temple jutting forth from the earth, like 'the nipple-peak on the breast of the Goddess of Freedom'. When he got the place dug and excavated, however, there was no Kāmalate. But before him stood the closed door of a shrine. Careless of consequence, Allama kicked the door open, and entered. He saw before him a yōgi in a trance, concentrated on the liṅga. His eyes and face were all aglow, his locks glowing, a garland of rudrākṣi seeds[1] round his neck, serpent ear-rings on his ears. Like the All-giving Tree, he sat there in the heart of the temple. The yōgi's name was Animiṣayya (the One without eyelids, the open-eyed one). While Allama stood there astonished, Animiṣayya gave into his hand a liṅga. Even as he handed over the liṅga, Animiṣayya's life went out. In that moment of transference, Allama became enlightened, and wandered henceforth where the Lord called him and where the Lord took him.

This experience of the secret underground, the cave-temple, is what is probably celebrated in the name Guhēśvara or Lord of Caves, which appears in almost every Allama vacana.

Other vacana saints recognized him instantly as the Master. Basavaṇṇa, Mahādēvi, Cennabasava, Siddharāma, Muktāyakka and others considered him their guru. Basava was known as *Aṇṇa* 'elder brother', Mahādēvi as *Akka* 'elder sister', but Allama was *Prabhu* or Master to everyone. A later poet, Cāmarasa, devoted an entire work *Prabhuliṅgalīle* to the Master's life, miracles and teachings. The *Śūnyasaṁpādane* or 'the Achievement of Nothingness', an important source for Vīraśaiva thought and poetry, was written round the life

1. Sacred to Śiva, also used as prayer beads; serpents as ornaments are also characteristic of Śiva.

and work of Allama, and describes his encounters with contemporary saints. According to all accounts, Kalyāṇa was established as the rallying centre of Vīraśaiva saints by Allama's spiritual presence as much as by Basavaṇṇa's efforts as minister of state. The company of saints, presided over by Allama, came to be known as *anubhava maṇṭapa* or 'the mansion of Experience'.

Allama's rejection of external ritual and worship was most complete. In his encounters with Basavaṇṇa, Mahādēviyakka (cf. section-notes on them) and others he leads them to understand their own imperfect rejection of externals: he teases, probes, questions their integrity. He stresses Basavaṇṇa's temptations in the world to which he has yielded even though in good works. He mocks at Mahādēvi flaunting her nudity to the gaze of the world and yet covering herself with her tresses. The Vīraśaiva rejection of various occult practices of the time is best illustrated by the episode of Gōrakṣa. Gōrakṣa was the leader of Siddhas or occult practitioners in search of supernatural powers (probably not to be identified with Gorakhnātha dated between the ninth and twelfth century, the master of a medieval occult tradition in North India,[2] despite the similarity of name and other circumstances). Whatever be the historical truth of the legend, the significance is clear.

Siddhas were after Siddhis, or 'miraculous powers'. In the course of yogic practices, the yogi acquires inevitably certain occult powers, suspending various powers of nature:

> being one he becomes many, or having become many, becomes one again; he becomes visible or invisible; he goes, feeling no obstruction, to the further side of a wall or rampart or hill, as if through air; he penetrates up and down through solid ground, as if through

2. For a succinct account of Siddhas cf. M. Eliade's *Yoga: Immortality and Freedom*, New York, 1958, pp. 301–7.

water; he walks on water without breaking through, as if on solid ground; he travels cross-legged in the sky, like the birds on the wing; even the Moon and the Sun . . . does he touch and feel with his hand; he reaches in the body even up to the heaven Brahama . . .[3]

While such powers are essential indications of the saint's progressive release from the conditions of earthly existence, they are also temptations to power, tempting the yogi to a vain magical mastery of the world (Eliade's phrase).[4] Both Hindu and Buddhist doctrines warn the novice against these temptations on the way to *samādhi* or *nirvāṇa*, or 'release'. Allama's magical contest with and victory over Gōrakṣa is symbolic of Vīraśaivism's rebuke to occult practices.

Gōrakṣa, the leader of the Siddhas, had a magical body, invulnerable as diamond. Allama mocked at his body, his vanity. Legend says that he gave Allama a sword and invited him to try cutting his body in two. Allama swung the sword at him, but the sword clanged on the solid diamond-body of Gōrakṣa; not a hair was severed. Gōrakṣa laughed in pride. Allamaprabhu laughed at this show-off and returned the sword, saying, 'Try it on me now.' Gōrakṣa came at Allama with his sword with all his strength. The sword swished through Allama's body as if it were mere space. Such were Allama's powers of self-emptying, his 'achievement of Nothingness'. Gōrakṣa was stunned – he felt acutely the contrast between his own powers and Allama's true realization, between his own diamond-body in which the carnal body had become confirmed and Allama's body which was no body but all spirit. This revelation was the beginning of his enlightenment. Allama said to him:[5]

3. From a buddhist text quoted by Eliade, op. cit., p. 178.
4. ibid., p. 177.
5. *Śūnyasaṁpādane*, ed. S. S. Bhoosnurmath, Dharwar, 1958, p. 449.

With your alchemies,
you achieve metals,
but no essence.

With all your manifold yogas,
you achieve
a body, but no spirit.

With your speeches and arguments
you build chains of words
but cannot define the spirit.

If you say
you and I are one,
you were me
but I was not you.

Legend describes Allama's perfect interiorization: To men living and dying in lust, he taught the divine copulation of yogic practice; to alchemists, he brought the magical inward drop of essence that transmuted the base metal of fear; to holy men living in the fearful world, exploiting trees for clothing, stripping root and branch in their hunger, drinking up river and lake in their thirst, Allama taught the spirit's sacrifice, converting them from the practice of animal sacrifice to the sacrifice of bestial self.

Thus by mockery, invective, argument, poetry, loving kindness and sheer presence, Allama brought enlightment to laymen, and release to the saints themselves.

Allama's vacanas say little of his early life, passions or conflicts. His vacanas were all uttered after he reached full enlightenment. Unlike others (e.g. Basavaṇṇa), he leaves few traces of early struggle or his biographical past. In a saint like Allama, 'the butterfly has no memory of the caterpillar'.

According to some, such an image of Allama, untempted and undivided by human passions, is a censored image, clipped and presented by scholars who love absolutes.

Allama's vacanas have been distributed in the Basavarāju edition (*Allamana Vacana Candrike*, Mysore, 1960) as follows:

Preliminary vacanas	1–63
Bhakta	64–112
Māhēśvara	113–156
Prasādi	157–173
Prāṇaliṅgi	174–310
Śaraṇa	311–606
Aikya	606–1321

(including songs set to music 1289–1321)

The overwhelming impression that Allama leaves of masterful wisdom and awareness without lapses is clearly reflected in the proportions of his vacanas in the different phases, or sthalas: over half the vacanas are about the later steps of the saint's ascent, the largest number are about the state of union and realization. Compare these proportions with those of Basavaṇṇa, where the greatest number is in the first bhakta-stage.

42

Look here,
the legs are two wheels;
the body is a wagon
full of things.

Five men[66] drive
the wagon
and one man is not
like another.

Unless you ride it
in full knowledge of its ways
the axle
will break,
O Lord of Caves.

59

Where was the mango tree,
where the koilbird?[67]

when were they kin?

Mountain gooseberry[68]
and sea salt:
when
were they kin?

and when was I
kin to the Lord
of Caves?

95

A little bee born
in the heart's lotus
flew out and swallowed
the sky.
        In the breeze
of his wing, three worlds
turned upside down.
                When
the cage of the five-coloured swan
was broken, the bee fell
to the ground with broken wings.

Living among your men,
O Lord of Caves,
  I saw the lovely tactic
of truth's coming on.[69]

101

I saw:
  heart conceive,
    hand grow big with child;
  ear drink up the smell
      of camphor, nose eat up
  the dazzle of pearls;
    hungry eyes devour
  diamonds.
          In a blue sapphire
  I saw the three worlds
    hiding,
      O Lord of Caves.[70]

109

If mountains shiver in the cold
with what
will they wrap them?

If space goes naked
with what
shall they clothe it?

If the lord's men become worldlings
where will I find the metaphor,

O Lord of Caves

211

I saw an ape tied up
at the main gate of the triple city,
taunting
every comer.

When the king came
with an army,
he broke them up at one stroke
and ate them.

He has a body, no head, this ape:
legs without footsteps,
hands without fingers;
a true prodigy, really.

Before anyone calls him, he calls them.
I saw him clamber over the forehead of the wild elephant
born in his womb
and sway in play
in the dust of the winds.

I saw him juggle his body as a ball
in the depth of the sky,
play with a ten-hooded snake
in a basket; saw him blindfold
the eyes of the five virgins.
I saw him trample the forehead
of the lion that wanders in the ten streets,
I saw him raise the lion's eyebrows.
I saw him grow from amazement
to amazement, holding a diamond
in his hand.

Nothing added,
nothing taken,

the Lord's stance
is invisible
to men untouched
by the Liṅga of the Breath.[71]

213

With a whole temple
in this body
where's the need
for another?

No one asked
for two.

O Lord of Caves,
if you are stone,
what am I?

218

They don't know the day
is the dark's face,
and the dark the day's.

A necklace of nine jewels
lies buried, intact, in the face of the night;
in the face of day a tree
with leaves of nine designs.

When you feed the necklace
to the tree,
the Breath enjoys it
in the Lord of Caves.[72]

219

It's dark above the clutching hand.
It's dark over the seeing eye.
It's dark over the remembering heart.
It's dark here
            with the Lord of Caves
            out there.

277

When the toad
swallowed the sky,
look, Rāhu
the serpent mounted
and wonder of wonders!
the blind man
caught the snake.

Thus, O Lord,
I learned
without telling the world.[73]

299

I heard the dead rooster crow
that the cat[74] devoured.
I saw the black koil come
and eat up the sun.
The casket burned and left
only the sacred thread.

The Liṅga of the Breath
breaks all rules
and grows unorthodox.

No one may trace
the footstep on the water;
the sound of the word
Guhēśvara*
is neither here
nor there.

* Lord of Caves

316

What's this darkness
on the eyes?
this death on the heart?
this battlefield within,
this coquetry without,
this path familiar to the feet?

319

A wilderness grew
in the sky.[75]
In that wilderness
a hunter.
In the hunter's hands
a deer.

The hunter will not die
till the beast
is killed.

Awareness is not easy,
is it,
O Lord of Caves?

396

I was
as if the fire in the tree
burned the tree

as if the sweet smells
of the winds of space
took over the nostrils

as if the doll of wax
went up in flames

I worshipped the Lord
and lost the world.

429

When the honey-bee came
I saw the smell[76] of flowers
run.

O what miracles!

Where the heart went
I saw the brain
run.

When the god came,
I saw the temple run.

431

Outside city limits
a temple.
In the temple, look,
a hermit woman.

In the woman's hand
a needle,
at needle's end
the fourteen worlds.

O Lord of Caves,
I saw an ant
devour whole
the woman, the needle,
the fourteen worlds.[77]

451

Show me once
the men

who have cut the guts
of the eye

roasted the kernels
of the heart

and learned
the beginnings
of the word

O Lord of Caves.[78]

459

The world tires itself thinking
it has buried all shadow.

Can shadows die
for limbed animals?

If you rage and curse here
at the thief out there
on the other shore,
will he just drop dead?

These men, they do not know
the secret,
the stitches of feeling;
would our Lord of Caves
come alive
just because they wish it?

461

For a wedding of dwarfs
rascals beat the drums
and whores
carry on their heads
holy pitchers;

with hey-ho's and loud hurrahs
they crowd the wedding party
and quarrel over flowers and betelnuts;

all three worlds are at the party;
what a rumpus this is,
without our Lord of Caves.

492

O Happening that never happened,
O Extremist Character,
why get worshipped
at the hands
of the dying?

O Lord of Caves,
it's a shame
to get worshipped
at the hands
of men
who get hurt
and die.

532

A tree[79] born
in a land without soil,
and look!
eight flowers
thunderbolt-coloured.
Fruit on the branch
ripen at the root.

O Lord of Caves,
only he is truly your man
who has eaten
of fruit fallen
loose from the stalk
in places no eye has seen:

only he,
no one else.

537

The fires of the city[80] burned in the forest,
forest fires burned in the town.
Listen, listen to the flames
of the four directions.
Flapping and crackling in the vision
a thousand bodies dance in it
and die countless deaths,

O Lord of Caves.

541

He's powerful, this policeman!
broke off the hands and feet of water
lopped off the nose and ears of fire
beheaded the winds
and impaled the sky on a stake.[81]

Destroyed the king and his two ministers.

Closed and shot the bolts of the nine gates
and locked them up
killed nine thousand men
till he was left alone

our Lord of Caves.

550

Poets of the past
are the children of my concubines.
Poets to come
are infants of my pity.
The poets of the sky
are babies in my cradle.

Viṣṇu and Brahma
are my kinsmen and sidekicks.

You are the father-in-law
and I the son-in-law,

O Lord of Caves.[82]

556

If it rains fire[83]
  you have to be as the water;

if it is a deluge of water
  you have to be as the wind;

if it is the Great Flood,
  you have to be as the sky;

and if it is the Very Last Flood of all the worlds,
  you have to give up self

and become the Lord.

616

Who can know green grass flames
  seeds of stone

  reflections of water
  smell of the wind

  the sap of fire
  the taste of sunshine on the tongue[84]

  and the lights in oneself

except your men?

629

One dies,
another bears him to the burial ground:
still another takes them both
and burns them.

No one knows the groom
and no one the bride.
Death falls across
the wedding.

Much before the decorations fade
the bridegroom is dead.

Lord, only your men
have no death.

634

In the mortar without water,[85]
pestles without shadows.

Women without bodies
pound rice without grains,

and sing lullabies
to the barren woman's son.

Under streamers of fire,
plays the child of the Lord.

668

The wind sleeps
to lullabies of sky.

Space drowses,
infinity gives it suck
from her breast.

The sky is silent.
The lullaby is over.

The Lord is
as if He were not.[86]

675

Light
devoured darkness.

I was alone
inside.

Shedding
the visible dark

I
was Your target

O Lord of Caves.

699

Sleep, great goddess sleep,
heroine of three worlds,
spins and sucks up
  all, draws breath
  and throws them down
  sapless.

I know of no hero
  who can stand before her.
  Struck by her arrows,
  people rise and fall.

775

A running river
  is all legs.

A burning fire
  is mouths all over.

A blowing breeze
  is all hands.

So, lord of the caves,
for your men,
every limb is Symbol.

802

Whoever knew
that It is body of body,

breath of breath
and feeling of feeling?

Thinking that it's far,
it's near,
it's out here
and in there,

they tire themselves out.

809

Some say
they saw It.
What is It,
the circular sun,
the circle of the stars?

The Lord of Caves
lives in the town
of the moon mountain.

836

For all their search
  they cannot see
  the image in the mirror.

It blazes in the circles
  between the eyebrows.
  Who knows this
  has the Lord.

959

Feed the poor
tell the truth
make water-places
for the thirsty
and build tanks for a town –

  you may then go to heaven
  after death, but you'll get nowhere
  near the truth of Our Lord.

And the man who knows Our Lord,
he gets no results.

966

For the wildfire, the forest is the target;
for the waterfire[87], the water;
for the body's fire, the body;
for death's conflagration, the worlds
  are target;

for the angry fire of your men, all men of ill-will;

yet for your illusion's lashing flames
  I'm no target, O Lord of Caves.

972

Looking for your light,
I went out:

it was like the sudden dawn
of a million million suns,

a ganglion of lightnings
for my wonder.

O Lord of Caves,
if you are light,
there can be no metaphor.

APPENDIX I

The Six-Phase System

(*Ṣaṭsthala Siddhānta*)

A RATHER esoteric intellectual system underlies the native arrangement of vacanas. Though not strictly relevant for the appreciation of vacana poetry, such a system is one of the many 'contexts' of these texts.

The vacanas and later Vīraśaiva texts in Kannada and Sanskrit speak of the mystical process as a succession of stages, a ladder of ascent, a metamorphosis from egg to larva to pupa to the final freedom of winged being. Often the devotee in his impatience asks to be cut loose from these stages of metamorphosis as in Mahādēvi 17.

Six phases or steps (*sthala*, *sōpāna*) are recognized. The devotee at each stage has certain characteristics; each stage has a specific relationship between the *aṅga* or the soul and the *liṅga* or the Lord. Liṅga creates all of creation out of no purpose, for it has no desires; so creation is described as Līlā or the Lord's play. The Lord's creative power is known as Māyā or Śakti, often translated as Illusion. Creation comes into being by the lord's engagement (*pravṛtti*); liberation for the aṅga is attained through disengagement (*nivṛtti*). The description of the first is a cosmology, not very different from the Śāṅkhya philosophy. The description of the disengagement is in the form of the Six phases. Māyā or Śakti creates desire and engagement not only for all creation but for each individual creature; bhakti ('devotion'), love for the Liṅga, is the counter-move. Bhakti disengages the creature from Māyā, and takes him step by step nearer to the Liṅga till he becomes one with him. Both śakti and bhakti are therefore powers of the Lord, moves and countermoves, not different from one another except in direction; one evolves, another devolves; one breathes in, the other breathes out.

The Liṅga has six *sthalas* or phases; the aṅga or creature has a corresponding six. These are best displayed in two corresponding diagrams, with somewhat rough glosses:

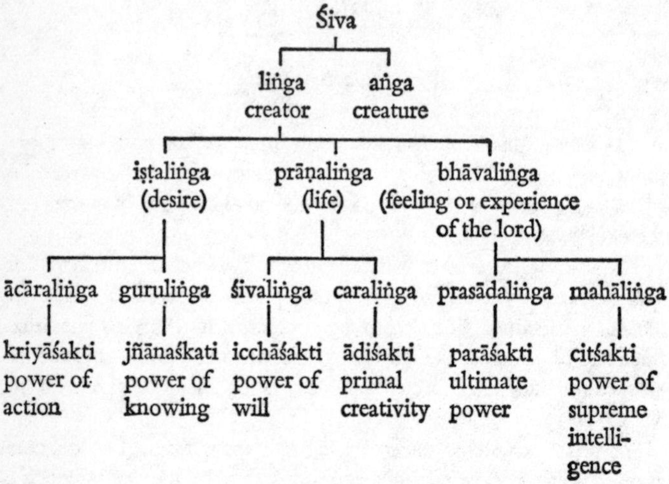

Aspects of Liṅga (the Lord)

Note that each of the liṅgas (aspects of the creator) is associated with a specific śakti, a motive for evolution, just as each of the aṅgas (stages of the creature) has a specific bhakti, a motive for disengagement.

From left to right, we see a hierarchic arrangement for śakti as well as well as for bhakti. In the liṅga diagram, it is probably better to speak of the various liṅgas and their attendant śaktis as *aspects* in the order of importance; for the aṅga, they are *stages*. One may also observe here that the tree-arrangement is by binary oppositions. In the first branch, it is liṅga *v.* aṅga. In the second branching, it is a combination of two oppositions, a Hegel-like dialectical triad. In diagram 1, it is (*iṣṭa* and *prāṅa*) *v. bhāva*, representing the opposition of Life in the World (Desire and Life) and the Life in the Lord (Experience of God). In diagram 2, it is (*tyāga* and

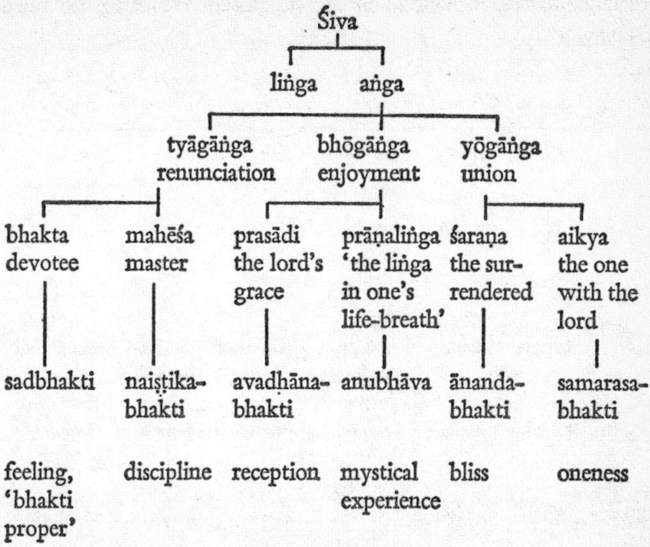

Stages of Aṅga (human soul)

bhōga) v. yoga, the opposition of the means in the world (Renunciation and Enjoyment) to the end beyond (Union with the Lord). It is obvious that the members of the two triads, like all the members of the final sestets, correspond to one another precisely: as the identity of aṅga and liṅga would require. Such identity is the beginning of creation as it is the 'end' of the creature; all differentiations (and diagrams) are only in the middle.

Further, the last six-way branch is the result of binary divisions under each of the previous three. The two members of each binary are related to each other as complements: *kriyā/jñāna* or doing/knowing; *icchā/ādi* or will/primal creation; *parā/cit* or the ultimate power/the ultimate intelligence in diagram 1; *sadbhakti/naiṣṭikabhakti* or devotion/discipline; *avadhāna/anubhāva* or receiving/experiencing; *ānanda/samarasa* or bliss/harmonious union in diagram 2. In some texts these six are made to correspond with six inner organs (*antaḥkaraṇa*) and the six outer organs of classical Hindu psychology; the latter correspond (somewhat asymmetrically) to the five elements. These correspondences, including the aṅga/liṅga sets, are best expounded in table form:

The elements	*Outer Senses*	*Inner Senses*	*Śakti-type*	*Liṅga-type*	*Sthala Phase*	*Kind of Bhakti*
Earth	smell	*citta*	*kriyā* or action	*ācāra*	*bhakti*	*śraddha* or *sad-bhakti*
Water	taste	*buddhi*	*jñāna* or knowing	*guru*	*mahēś-vara*	*niṣṭhe*
Fire	sight	*ahaṅ-kāra*	*icchā* or will	*Śiva*	*prasādi*	*avadhāna*
Air	touch	*manas*	*ādi* or primal power	*jaṅgama*	*prāṅa-liṅgi*	*anubhāva*
Sky or Space	hearing	*jñāna*	*parā* or ultimate power	*prasāda*	*śaraṇa*	*ānanda*
Sky or Space	heart(?)	*bhāva*	*cit* or supreme intelli-gence	*mahā*	*aikya*	*samarasa*

Some would add to this table a set of corresponding *cakras* or centres of power in the human body, a hierarchy or route of ascent for the life-force beginning with the peritonium through the genitals, umbilicus, heart, neck, between-the-eyes, and the crown of the head. Reaching the last would result in union with the supreme reality, aikya or samarasa according to the Vīraśaiva chart.

We should say a little more about the phases of bhakti, the 'stages of Life's way' for the devotee. These stages, described by an expert theologian of the movement, Cennabasava, fit remarkably well the actual stages of each saint's development. It is a convenient typology of saints' legends. The poems in our selection, following the Kannada editions, are arranged according to this six-phase order (cf. section-introductions to Basavaṇṇa, Dāsimayya and Allama pp. 65, 95, 148).

1. In the bhakta-phase he practises bhakti (devotion) and worships ācāraliṅga, which is attended by kriyāsakti or the power of action. Example: Basavaṇṇa 59.

2. In the next phase, he moves from bhakti to niṣṭhe or discipline. This is a phase of endurance, or ordeals and temptations. Poems in this phase, like Basavaṇṇa 563, lash out against the unregenerate and the unfaithful, often ambiguously addressed to oneself as well as to other sinners.

3. The third phase, prasādi, is more peaceful than the second. In this phase, the devotee realizes that he is secure in the Lord's keep and sees his workings everywhere. All things are offerings, all acts acts of devotion. The very senses that tempted the devotee by their blandishments become sites for the Lord's six-fold presence: the six aspects of the Liṅga are distributed through the six senses.

'The nostrils are ācāraliṅga
The tongue is guruliṅga
The eyes are śivaliṅga
The tongue is jaṅgamaliṅga
The ears are prasādaliṅga,
And feeling (bhāva) is mahāliṅga . . . thus your devotee receives the Lord in every limb,' says Cennabasava. Each sense dedicates its special experience as its offering: the nostrils their sense of the world's smells, the eyes vision, the tongue its taste, etc. Thus are the senses transformed. So is the world of experience. In this stage, no explicit offering need be made. For 'sound, touch, shape, taste, smell and the five senses move constantly towards the liṅga. Each [sense] knows its enjoyment is all for the Lord and towards Him' (Cennabasava). 'When the ground turns policeman where can the burglar run? Is there anything held back from the man whose every limb is Liṅga?' Before they touch one's senses, sensations are already dedicated to the Liṅga. For in this stage, the Lord is 'the hearing ear in the ear, the seeing eye in the eye'. One's limbs and senses are Śiva's limbs, Śiva's senses. Thus I becomes Thou. His acts cease to be karma, they cannot smear him. This bhakti is avadhāna or 'receiving'.

4. In the next stage, avadhāna ('receiving') gives place to anubhāva ('experiencing'), for the devotee moves from the outer world to the inner. Seeing Śiva in all things, he is filled with compassion. As all things are offerings, he 'fasts, partaking of a feast,' 'uses pleasure and yet is virgin' (Basavaṇṇa). In the above three, the actions of the bhakta are still important; in the next three his awareness becomes

primary. So far, he is a novitiate, disciplining body and mind, controlling their distractions, making the outer inner. In the fourth stage or prānaliṅgi (devoted to the liṅga in the breath) the devotee turns inward. His heart is cleansed, his intelligence clear, his ego and senses stilled, he begins to see the light of the Lord in himself. For the Liṅga of the Breath (*prāṇaliṅga*), 'the body is the altar, its ritual bath is in the Ganges of the sky, it worships with fragrance without flowers. In the heart's lotus, the sound of *Śiva Śiva*. Such is oneness, O Lord of Caves' (Allama).

5. In the fifth stage, he is with the Lord and suffers only as a loving woman suffers her lover's absence, living in two worlds, half-mad, half in a coma, 'a fool of god'. Many of Mahādēvi's vacanas belong to this phase: e.g. 79, 120. In this śaraṇasthala, he knows he is not contained in his skin, nor made of earth, water, air, fire, and space, nor a thing of the five senses.

6. As Śiva and Śakti are primordially one, śarana and Liṅga become one. There is no worship any more, for who is out there to receive such worship? This is Oneness or *aikyasthala*. Like space joining space, water water, the devotee dissolves nameless in the Lord, who is not another.

Characteristically, the devotee believes that all schemes may dissolve and all stages may merge. The vacanakāras say that in any one *sthala* all other *sthalas* are inherent; that the six stages may only be a manner of speaking of the unspeakable, an ascent on the ladder with no rungs.

On the other hand, later theologians with their penchant for systems have given each phase six sub-phases, each sub-phase further phases and detail as many as 216 stages in life's way. But such excesses need not detain us and are inimical to the true vacana-spirit.

As some of the considerations of the six phases of the 'pilgrim's progress' illuminate certain vacanas, we have offered, in the introduction to each section, a chart of each saint's vacanas classified according to the six-phase system. Such classifications are traditional, and do not fit everywhere. But they make, if nothing else, a useful index of themes.

APPENDIX II

On Lingayat Culture

by William McCormack

Lingayats are members of a Kannada-speaking caste-sect of southern India who qualify, by virtue of wearing on their bodies the symbol (*liṅga*) of their god Śiva, to receive His blessings. A modern attempt was made to show Lingayats as having a religion separate from 'Hindu' when 'Lingayats' received discrete entry in the Indian Constitution of 1950. But we believe Lingayats to be Hindus because their beliefs are syncretistic and include an assemblage of many Hindu elements, including the name of their god, Śiva, who is one of the chief figures of the Hindu pantheon. A. K. Ramanujan documents this point in his introduction to the present book, where he discusses Hindu symbolic elements in *vacanas*.

It is true that the Lingayat founding prophet, Basavaṇṇa, preached against Hindu caste in his vacanas and seemingly attacked the religious and secular mediator role of Brahmans, who are Hinduism's hereditary caste of priests. But Lingayats today, like other Hindus, accommodate to teachings of Hinduism which hold the terms 'Brahmanism' and 'Hinduism' to be interchangeable, and place Brahman priests at the head of society, its social as well as its religious leaders, and its models for personal and moral worth. If this fact of a Hindu's unquestioned acceptance of the honourable precedence of Brahman priests above 'ordinary' men is fully grasped, then we can better understand how close religion is to the Hindu's perception of his combined social and personal self. As a Hindu, one does not readily admit to one's own lack of understanding of the Brahman's beliefs and religious practices. Such an admission would be a kind of sin. At the same time, it would also amount to an admission of social incompetence, for acknowledgement of imperfection in these matters would be to lower oneself on a ladder of personal worth which derives its symbols of moral success always from what Brahmans have already ostensibly achieved. Caste thus sets very severe limits to human understanding and the expression of personal interests and inner feelings. It is this limitation on self-expression, set by the multitude of rules of 'correct' behaviour appropriate to one's hereditary caste station in life, that Indian poets and prophets like Basavaṇṇa reacted against. In reporting their inner emotional experiences to others, they often effectually symbolize a freedom of emotional life about which ordinary persons may only dream. For Basavaṇṇa, caste exacted too high a price in terms of individual development and feelings of independence for the self – a price which Basavaṇṇa and other medieval and modern Indian poets have been spiritually unwilling or unable to pay. The rank and file of Lingayats, on the other hand, have been less able to resist the all-encompassing socio-cultural mesh of Brahmanism: 'As in the case of Christianity in some parts of India, the social barriers of caste have proved too strong for the... orthodox [Lingayat] religion' ('Lingayats', in *Encyclopaedia of Religion and Ethics*, Scribner's Sons, New York, 1909).

Basavaṇṇa's importance in the Kannada country has been verified in the archaeology of the region, for inscriptions have been deciphered which mention his life in the twelfth century. No inscription mentions the other writers whom Lingayats believe to have been Basavaṇṇa's contemporaries. Thus Basavaṇṇa's putative nephew is singled out in the above-mentioned article as 'perhaps only a mythical person'. Similarly, there are no contemporary biographies of Allama Prabhu, who perhaps taught philosophical monism through his vacanas. Nor is there a biography of Akkamma (Mahādēvi), a female ascetic and mystic associated with the Śrīśaila shrine in the Telegu-speaking region of South India. 'Akkamma' means 'respected elder sister', and she is recognized in popular lithographs by her absence of clothing save for a hair cloak. We lack documentation for the details of even Basavaṇṇa's life.

Lacking information on the lives of these saints, I attempted an effort to ascertain their emotional attitudes and outlooks by analysis of the content of their writings, and thus made a frequency count of selected categories of metaphors in vacanas attributed to Basavaṇṇa, Allama Prabhu, and Mahādēvi. The categories chosen were metaphors about animals, about persons, about natural objects (including plants), and about objects of cultural interest (meaningful because local or Hindu traditions have selected them for attention, e.g., preference for one art style rather than another). The frequency count for a very large sample of Basavaṇṇa's vacanas revealed the pattern that his metaphors concerned either persons (nearly 50 per cent) or cultural categories (50 per cent), and practically excluded the other two categories. (For an adaptation of this method to computer technology, see B. N. Colby, 'Cultural Patterns in Narrative', *Science*, Vol. 151, 18 February 1966, pp. 793–8.) When Basavaṇṇa did very rarely select an animal metaphor, it pertained to the dog, an animal he apparently disliked. For Hindus, the dog is associated with impurity: it eats garbage and human faeces, and if a Hindu priest is bitten by a dog, he is forever disbarred from performing rituals for his clients. One can speculate that the dog symbolized impurity to Basavaṇṇa's unconscious as well, though at a conscious level he rejected the significance of impurity and rejected especially, according to Lingayat traditions, the Hindu beliefs about the impurity of women. On the other hand, an historical interpretation of Basavaṇṇa's dislike for dogs is equally interesting, in that the black dog cult of Śiva was in competition with early Lingayatism for the allegiance of Śiva worshippers. Yet a third interpretation of Hindu ambivalence about animals and women is the psychoanalytic one, and for this the reader is referred to E. Erikson's book on *Gandhi's Truth* (Faber & Faber, 1970).

Lingayats, sometimes styled as 'strict Śiva-devotees', or Vīraśaivas, were estimated to number nearly four million in 1959. They then constituted about 16 per cent of the total population of Mysore State, a Kannada-speaking state drawn in 1956 along linguistic lines according to the Indian States Reorganization Act of 1955. The general elections of 1957, 1962, and 1967 showed Lingayats to be the most popular and powerful political force in Mysore, due to their position as the single largest caste group, with a voting plurality, in the state. Before the 1956 state reorganization, state politics had been putatively controlled by the *Vokkaliga*, or 'farmer', caste, and Lingayats too were and are mainly farmers. But the reorganization of the state enlarged its territory by adding Kannada-speaking areas where Lingayats made up as much as 50 per cent of the population. Of Lingayat subcastes, the two largest are known by the names of occupations which only a minority can practise: the jaṅgamas, or priests, and the banajigas, or traders. The current president of the National Congress Party of India, Śrī Nijaliṅgappa, would trace his ethnic origins to the banajiga subcaste of Lingayats. Thus a social-science value to this book and to A. K. Ramanujan's explication of vacana symbolism is that we here make a beginning in communicatting certain universal aspects of symbols which give Lingayats a certain regional integration and historical continuity as a group.

In the southern districts of modern Mysore State, and especially in Mysore District itself where is situated the palace of the former princely ruler of the state, there is a tendency to regard jaṅgamas and aradhya (Śaiva) Brahmans as closely related if not identical castes. In these districts, priestly functions such as the ministration of life-cycle rituals – that is, the public ceremonies which mark the changes in the status and life-pattern of individuals (birth, marriage, death rituals) – may be performed for Lingayats by priests of either caste. The other major function of jaṅgamas pertains to Lingayats everywhere, and is not open to aradhya Brahmans: this is to provide most of the recruits for the Lingayat ascetic orders, especially for the order of the red-robed *virakta* monks. As is the case with Brahmanism generally, priests who officiate at life-cycle rituals may be married, but ascetics like the Lingayat *viraktas* are celibate, preside over their own monasteries, and do not perform birth, marriage, or death sacraments. *Viraktas* are not drawn exclusively from the jaṅgama subcaste, but there has been a tendency to favour recruiting boys from the priestly jaṅgama families – which are bound by that restriction against widow or divorcee remarriage which is generally felt to be a Brahman trait in southern India.

The chief occasions which traditionally require the presence of jaṅgama (or aradhya) priests are the ceremonies performed at the birth of a child, its naming about a fortnight after birth, the puberty maturation of a girl (first menstruation), marriage, and death. The audience for these life-crisis rituals is drawn from relatives, friends, and neighbours, so that no new friendships are established by these celebrations. It is a case of strengthening and reinforcing old acquaintances, and renewing the ties of blood and kin relationship. In the same way, the marriage contract negotiated by the parents of bridal couples tend toward the renewal of old kinship bonds, the preferred spouse among Kannada-speakers being a mother's brother's, or a father's sister's, child. Or, a mother's brother may wed his sister's daughter, thereby contracting a marriage which cross-cuts the 'generation gap'.

When a child is born, the father sends for that jaṅgama priest who serves the family by hereditary right, and the priest initiates the infant by ceremonially tying a liṅga to the child's body. Thus a child born to Lingayat parents is the recipient of full sectarian membership soon after his birth. On some occasions, usually at a Lingayat monastery, the initiation ceremony may be repeated in more elaborate form. Those who are not born Lingayats undergo this same ritual if they agree to perform a lifetime vow of strict vegetarianism. The cabalistic interpretation of liṅga-wearing is that the liṅga represents the wearer's soul, which is not different from the divinity, Śiva. Thus the personal liṅga is a small replica of the black stone image of Śiva found in temples. The liṅga worn by adults, however, is covered over with a black tar-like substance which hardens so that the whole resembles a robin's egg in shape and size, and is worn in a silver case suspended from the neck by a special cord to slightly above belt level.

When a boy receives the initiation rite in a monastery, it provides him with a kind of licence for priesthood, and as such the ceremony is slightly different for him and his peers. The ritual proceeds in three stages, and requires several hours for completion. First, the five founding fathers of Lingayat priestly lineages are worshipped in the form of five pots which have been ritually dressed and enthroned on a ceremonially cleaned place. If jaṅgama boys are being initiated, a string connects each with his own ancestral pot. In the second stage, the importance of the liṅga is dramatized by the chanting of Sanskrit magical formulae. Then the liṅga is tied to each initiate, and the sacred six syllables of Śiva are whispered into each candidate's ear. Finally, there is a period of advice on religious and social conduct, during which the group is lectured by the officiating teacher, who must be a celibate and has a special title (*pattadswamy*).

Water is prominent in the worship of Śiva, and in Lingayat rituals it is usually applied to the feet, especially the toes, of an officiating jaṅgama priest. Cabalistically, the worship of the jaṅgama's feet symbolizes the unity of the worshipper's inner self with the jaṅgama, and of all with the Holy Spirit of Śiva. The water itself is regarded as consecrated by these acts – like the water poured in worship of the liṅga in a Śiva temple, or the waters of the Ganges River. After the ritual address to the jaṅgama's feet, both he and the worshipper pour the consecrated water over their own liṅgas, held in the left hand. This water they drink, in the belief that it carries Śiva's blessing, as a Hindu would drink Ganges water or the temple 'liṅga water'.

Most Lingayat life-cycle rituals include worship of the priest's feet. Funerals present a practical difficulty, since the decedent, the principal actor in the ritual, cannot actively worship, but the difficulty is resolved by the priest's placing his foot on the head of the corpse. At weddings the bridal couple are themselves worshipped by participants as embodiments of Śiva and his heavenly consort Parvati, thus foot-worship and water ritual find no prominent place. Worship of the jaṅgama's feet is performed in the Lingayat's home on holidays forming part of the local festival calendar, on fortnights when the moon changes its course as between waxing and waning, on Mondays (Śiva's sacred day), and on special occasions at the will of the householder.

Jaṅgamas, like Brahman priests, serve as astrological advisers. They can also serve as matchmaker for their client families when those families are unrelated and the anticipated marriage is not to be between cousins or between an uncle and his niece.

Folksongs form an integral part of the Lingayat religion, and are not unrelated to life-cycle ceremonies. Women sing traditional songs at the first menstruation ceremony for a matured girl and at all stages of the marriage ritual, that is, on the day of betrothal, on the wedding day, on the day the marriage is consummated, and on Wednesdays and Saturdays in the respective houses of the bridal couple for one to five weeks after the marriage. Funerals are an occasion for male folk-singing, performed with more elaborate instrumental accompaniment and greater professionalism than female singing, by more or less permanent musical groups. The themes of female folksongs are in line with female interests: women sing from legends about Lingayat heroines, and in praise of the Goddess, who takes many forms including those of first cause of the universe (Śiva's mother) and Parvati (Śiva's wife). The folksongs also describe the delights of holidays and the psychology of family living. The same songs are sung when women are working at home or in the fields, at leisure in the evenings, carrying a coconut or other sacrificial offering to a temple or to graves of Lingayat saints or heroes, and so on. Singing groups include anyone who is available for the occasion and wishes to participate, thus they are mixed in age and made up of relatives, neighbours, and friends belonging to the same village, but women rarely visit other villages or towns to perform their folksongs. One popular folksong illustrates how themes of family psychology can be mixed with legend and symbolization of caste purity. This is the song which pits Parvati, Śiva's pure but dissatisfied wife, against his beloved mistress, Ganga ('water', mother of rivers, symbol of fertility, shown iconographically in association with Śiva's head), who is quiet and beautiful but was born to a very low caste status. The pattern of village prostitution does draw women from low castes to serve men of higher birth, so there is a note of realistic feminine jealousy in this situation. The folksong first presents Parvati ridiculing Ganga's low birth and scorning Ganga's dietary habits of allegedly eating fish and crocodile, for, as a member of a fisher and ferryman caste, Ganga does presumably eat non-vegetarian, therefore ritually 'unclean', food. Parvati then imagines the sorry spectacle of Ganga in working dress carrying a basket of stinking fish on her head. Śiva is upbraided for his loss of wisdom in bringing such a girl into the family, and is even accused of having made the mistake without benefit of free will: 'It is written in fate that you will catch the feet of a dirty girl.' Finally, Parvati complains that Śiva has brought this tongue-tied Ganga from a low social position and placed her, however impure, in a position of superiority over herself, the legal wife.

The folksong performances of male singers are much more organized affairs, for the groups often have leaders and choral arrangements, and the occasion and purpose of the singing are more defined. But there is also a recreational aspect to male folk-singing, or *bhajana*, and the more professional male groups receive travel expenses from the organizers of religious fairs, festivals, and processions in diverse villages and towns. Because vacanas enjoy wide public interest and often have professional status, men perform them more frequently than do women. The relatively simple language of some of the vacana lyrics lend themselves to singing, but the structures and sense of longer sentences is sometimes broken by the requirements of melodic line and repetition. Similar alterations of the vacana texts occur when the few classical artists who sing them perform over local radio or in concerts.

Another type of cultural performance is the readings of purana stories in praise of Lingayat saints and deities, and this inspires gatherings in the Lingayat monasteries every evening during the holy month of 'Shravana' (July–August). In a modern-oriented monastery, the evening purana programme may include items of contemporary interest, such as the dedication of a Lingayat author's book or a musical performance. But there will also be purana stories about nineteenth- and twentieth-century Lingayat saints. For example, one of these concerns the *virakta* Hangal Kumarswamy, who was active in organizing educational institutions and free boarding clubs to assist rural students in gaining modern education. The traditional purana themes, like the folksongs, are more concerned with praising saints and deities in order to win symbolic merit for the audience, and with advising people on the perennial problems in family psychology. The specialist's skill in purana performance consists, not in reading the text aloud – an assistant often does that – but in explaining and making relevant to the lives of the assembled persons the passage which is read out. Most Lingayat puranas are written in a six-line verse form, and one stanza, or as little as two to four lines, is read out and explained, often at great length, before another section is taken up. In a month's reading, perhaps 25 to 35 per cent of the written text will be covered. Along with *prabacan*, which is a much simpler performance and not limited to exposition of one text, the purana readings ritually express a distinct Lingayat theosophy. This mystical doctrine is usually explained in terms of the 'six principles' (*shatsthala*) for individual spiritual development, and Lingayats feel that it ranks with any that Brahmanism has produced. Indeed, according to the Lingayat Sanskrit scholar, Dr S. C. Nandimath (*Handbook of Vīraśaivism*, Dharwar, 1941), there are philosophical similarities with the monism preached by the eighth-century Vedantin, Sankaracharya.

For the average villager, the most concrete and therefore the most meaningful manifestations of Lingayat ritual are the several religious fairs which are celebrated to honour Lingayat saints and heroes. These fairs, held mainly during the slack season for agriculture and during Shravana, provide an opportunity for individuals, *bhajana* singing groups, and whole families to vacation away from the village. Besides enjoying relief from the village pressures for conformity, some villagers bring oxen to these meets and engage in trade. The main business of fairs is a religious procession, for which an image or picture of the deity or saint in whose name the fair is held is placed in a chariot, usually a four-wheeled wooden vehicle with a tower-like superstructure. The date of the fair is fixed by calendar, but the exact time of the procession is fixed by astrological calculation, in the belief that spiritual beings draw the chariot which only seems to move by human traction. Thus procession time is a very lucky time to be at the place of procession, and a tremendous flocking of pilgrims characterizes the scene, in a way that is analogous, though on smaller scale, to the crowding to reach the confluence of the Ganges and Jumna rivers at Allahabad during the world-famous Kumbha Mela fair. Several smaller processions with *bhajana* accompaniment go along with the main chariot, and may also receive offerings and honour from the crowd as they pass. Ahead of the chariot stretch many groups of drummers and dancers, costumed to represent legendary figures of Śiva's heavenly court. In front of the chariot, teams of men carry one or more tall flag poles, which are believed to have protective power for what comes behind, so that there is a competitive show of devotion by the pole-bearers to carry the heavy pole recklessly forward alone and unassisted for some few yards. Usually water is poured on the ground before the chariot to ritually purify the ground and show honour, and the image in the chariot receives food-offerings and honour from the waving of burning oil lamps that are affixed to the platters of food. The platters are carried to the chariot by women, but priestly attendants receive the offerings to the image – as they would do in a temple – and these priestly mediators then return a portion of the offerings to the givers.

On the occasion of a fair, sacrificial offerings are made also to any near and relevant temple deity, usually at dawn, in late afternoon, or in early evening. There are stalls at the religious fairs for the sale of ritual articles, like liṅgas, the white ash (*vibhuti*) which Śiva-worshippers wear on the forehead, or religious beads (the so-called 'Śiva's eyes', or *rudrakshi* beads). Besides these, there are food and drink stalls, as also publishers' stalls selling pictures of the saints and deities, framed or unframed, and various popular books and religious pamphlets at prices ranging from a quarter of a rupee to as much as seven or eight rupees for the larger astrological handbooks. The ten- to seventy-page pamphlets are produced for purely commercial sale by twenty or so small family firms, and are regularly available on railway platforms, from street-pedlars on market day, and from the small book stalls in the bazaars. The same or similar materials are published by several different firms, so that a would-be purchaser will not have difficulty in finding a popular item. The category of popular books includes the larger collections of vacanas and the more complete printed texts of purana stories, whereas pamphlets include only fragments. It is the more educated and sophisticated people who form the audience for the popular books, and they obtain them from the publishers, from monasteries (which often are publishers for the longer puranas), and in a few general bookstores which typically sell also English publications and Kannada novels.

Women do not serve on the committees which manage the fairs, nor on the various temple and monastery trust committees as a rule, but women do sponsor cultural performances through their own 'Akkamma' or 'Big Sister' clubs. These are mainly urban phenomena, and one of their main interests, the advancement of women's education, is an urban idea. Another, closely related, interest is the protection of female orphans. To this end women arrange for the marriages of nubile orphans, and feed, clothe, and house orphans with the help of state grants allotted to 'orphanages'. Folk-singing is a regular adjunct to a women's club meeting, but many of these songs derive their themes from participation in the new national life in India, and some may be in Hindi. Besides Hindi, some clubs teach handiwork, as inspired by Gandhian idealism, and regularly conduct public celebrations of Gandhi's birthday and the new local holidays (*nadhabba*, so-called 'district festivals') which symbolize patriotism. In at least three cities, the Akkamma clubs provide nursery-school services.

The strongest forces in Lingayat educational development have been the *virakta* monks, who have been active in this field since 1900 and whose efforts have had general impact since 1920. The main thrust of their efforts at organization has been towards providing free boarding hostels in places where high schools and colleges can service village boys. In a few cases the monks have started their own colleges and high schools, in cities as also in rural areas. State financial assistance is forthcoming for most of these efforts. In providing hostelry to village children, the monks not only give financial assistance – charity cases are handled from the general funds of the monasteries – but also provide a kind of social and human environment which the village parents and castemen approve of. The hostels are a kind of way-station to the more secular and interdenominational life of the urban universe, and in some cities, paying guests are so numerous at the hostel that it takes on the appearance of an American college dormitory. There are many more applicants than places in the dormitory, so screening hearings are held before admission is granted. This makes for a certain 'esprit de corps' among those admitted and also gives the students' experience more status value to the parents and their castemen. A nice balance has to be struck in these matters, however, as dormitories qualify for state assistance only if they are open to children of all castes and sects.

Thus alongside of the more traditional forms of Vīraśaiva religious communication described above – the life-cycle rituals, religious fairs, purana and folksong performances, and so forth – there has arisen a new form of sectarian communication that is more closely geared to contemporary Indian national educational and political institutions. One of the more significant new rituals is instruction and written examination over book-learned sectarian doctrine. This new type of 'initiation' ritual serves to rehearse individuals in educational processes for gaining positions in the state bureaucracy through merit achievement rather than by birth into a particular family and caste status. Any interpretation of the degree to which traditional birth-status criteria still play a role in recruitment to office, in spite of the modernist thrust of achievement orientation, is a difficult one, however, and the question of Lingayats *qua* Lingayats in education is fraught with nearly as many twists and turns and sensitivities to special privilege as the debates about state support to private schools in America. Ethnic politics generally operate in Mysore State through an informal and pragmatic control of elections and appointments by the dominant faction in the 'dominant caste' (i.e., the caste with the statewide plurality). Thus there is no 'caste state' to attract the criticism of a watchful public. But the official definition of 'social and educational backwardness' made in the late 1950s and early 1960s seems – even today, after a series of experiments and a Supreme Court decision (M. R. Balaji and others *versus* the State of Mysore, *All India Reporter*, 1963) – to double the ordinary chances of a Lingayat's gaining state aid in high school or college, or gaining admission to medical and engineering schools financed by the state. The present definition of 'backwardness' is that the income of the student's family not exceed an annual figure of Rupees 1,200, and to the watchful public, this seems a definition much subject to manipulation. Relatively little is known on the degree of Lingayats' involvement in Sanskritic philosophical learning, ordinarily exclusively a Brahman privilege in traditional Hinduism, which might show that an element of 'structural rivalry' had existed for a long time in prelude to the situation here described. It is known that in the nineteenth century, Lingayat and Brahman Sanskrit scholars (or Śastris) sometimes engaged in public challenges and debates, anticipating the present competition between Lingayats and Brahmans for top positions in the educational system. The traditional *shatsthāla* philosophy of Lingayats, referred to above and also explicated by A. K. Rámánujan in the Introduction, is often regarded by modernists as if it were a 'contraculture' (see Werner Stark, *The Sociology of Religion*, Vol. II, *Sectarian Religion*, Routledge & Kegan Paul, 1967, pp. 95, 129) to Brahmanist learning – in the fashion of sects everywhere – and its function does seem to be more to express sectarian competitiveness than to transmit a set of sectarian beliefs. This competition has been described for contemporary Mysore by several knowledgeable observers, including M. N. Srinivas, a leading anthropologist in India, who views the competition as a persistence of traditional caste attitudes (*Caste in Modern India and Other Essays*, Asia Publishing House, New York, 1962).

In conclusion, we have seen that the Lingayats are a numerous caste-sect, who are composed of several occupational subcastes of the Kannada-speaking country, and who have a particular stake in the worship of Śiva according to their own special views. Where the general psychology governing their religion touches on other than universals of human nature, it can be seen to be Hindu, though their belief in special features of their worship is strong, perhaps partly because wearing one's own personal liṅga is a kind of commitment that others, who only visit the liṅga representation in Śiva temples, do not have. A modern development in Lingayatism has been the group's commitment to secular educational achievement, especially as guided by the celibate *viraktas* who are today living out the paradox that, though ideally committed to a life of ascetic withdrawal from society, they are in fact leading the society towards modernization.

It does seem fitting that in the country where Gandhi, a 'mahatma' or religious figure, led the first drive for nationhood, monks prove to be the most successful in generating and mobilizing support for educational progress and social change. In addition, it can be noted that vacanas are today understood by many modernist Lingayats to have autobiographical significance; thus for some Lingayats the vacanas hold a position analogous to the position that Gandhi's *Autobiography* holds for some Gandhians. The point is that these writings set forth life-principles which exemplify ethical progress, and they could thus be made to serve as a solid foundation for a revitalization of Indian traditions and national identity. Those criteria for ethical progress sought by the Lingayat modernists in the vacanas, namely, humanism and universalism, are not significantly different from those proposed for modern anthropology by the Gandhian and anthropologist, Nirmal Kumar Bose (his *Cultural Anthropology*, Asia Publishing House, 1962, pp. 103–7).

The University of Calgary
30 September 1969 WILLIAM MCCORMACK

Notes to the Poems

These notes offer brief glosses on images, conventions, technical terms, ambiguities, subtleties of form or meaning in the Kannada original which the English translation could not quite convey. Cross-references to other poems, themes, and to relevant portions of the Introduction and the Appendixes, are also included. The numbers in the notes refer to vacana texts.

BASAVAṆṆA

1. The world as raging sea: a traditional metaphor, *Saṁsārasāgara*; *saṁsāra* is 'world', or 'life-in-the-world'. Basavaṇṇa was both statesman and saint, living in two worlds. In these and other poems he expresses the conflict of the two worlds.
2. *Lord of the meeting rivers: Kūḍalasaṅgamadēva*, a form of Śiva, Basavaṇṇa's chosen personal god. Kūḍalasaṅgama: a holy place in North Karnatak (South India) where two rivers meet. Basavaṇṇa first found enlightenment here.
   Almost every poem of Basavaṇṇa is addressed to Śiva as the lord of the meeting rivers. In this poem, the name is not just a formula or a signature line, but participates in the water-imagery of the poem.
3. *digit:* digits or phases of the moon.
4. *Rāhu:* the cosmic serpent of Indian mythology who devours the moon, causing eclipses.
5. The eclipse-image here, unlike the sea in 8, carries with it the hope of natural release (*mōkṣa*).
6. *The heart as monkey:* a traditional image for the restless distracted heart (*manas*). In Kannada, the word *mana* or *manas* could mean either heart and mind. cf. 36. In this and the previous poem, the Lord is the Father: a favourite stance of bhakti or personal devotion. Other stances are Lover/Beloved and Master/Servant.
7. *sensual bitches: karaṇēndriyaṅgaḷeṁba soṇaga. karaṇēndriya*'s are

the various faculties or sense-organs of mind (or heart, *manas*) and body. The *nine* sense-organs is a puzzle. The numbers differ in different texts. Here is an upaniṣadic list – the senses of apprehension are eye, ear, nose, tongue, skin; and the senses of performance are vocal organs for speech, hands for prehension, feet for locomotion, sex organ for procreation, and the organ of elimination of waste (S. K. Ramachandra Rao, *The Development of Indian Psychology*, Mysore, 1963, p. 22).

The poem uses forms of *manas* for what I have rendered as mind (l.9) and as heart (l.10). The heart is the quarry in this hunt.

8. The soul as a cow (*paśu*) in a quagmire: one of the attributes of Śiva is *paśupati*, the lord of beasts. *Paśu* in Kannada has a double sense of both 'cow or bull' and 'beast, creature'. The Tamil Śaiva doctrines speak of three elements: *paśu*, creature or creation, *pati*, the lord or creator, and *pāśam*, the attachment or love of the two. Vacana 52 makes indirect use of the threefold doctrine of *paśu-pati-pāśam*.

9. *your men: śarana*, a Vīraśaiva technical term, literally 'the ones who have surrendered (to god)'.

10. Like 33 and 36, 59 is also about the distractions of a worldling, struggling for oneness with the Lord. This struggle is related to the yogic ideal of 'stilling the waves of the mind', reducing the distractions of the senses.

11. In a world of disrelations, the devotee seeks relation and belonging. *Son of the house* (*maneya maga*) may be taken in the obvious sense, as a legitimate heir of the house, to express Basavaṇṇa's need for belonging. Or it may refer to the practice of rich masters and kings adopting servants as 'sons of the house' who lived inseparably with them, and committed ritual suicide when the masters died. Inscriptions of the period amply attest to the practice. M. Cidānandamurti in his Kannada book, *Kannaḍa śāsanagaḷa sāṁskṛtika adhyayana, The Cultural Study of Kannada Inscriptions* (Mysore, 1966), has a chapter on ritual suicide in the Kannada area (cf. especially pp. 306–7). In a footnote (312) he even makes the suggestion that the devotee's relation to the liṅga he wore on his body was that of a 'son of the house': when the liṅga was accidentally lost, the devotee often committed

suicide. Later saints condemn such excessive practices. In 62 the father/son and master/servant stances merge.

12. Ghosts are believed to stand guard over hidden treasure, though they cannot touch it. The rock/water relation is reversed in ghost/gold: the rock is not affected by water, but the ghost cannot affect the gold. The gold symbolizes the worldling's untouched spirit.

13. Vacanas are often ironic parables. cf. also 105, 111.

14. Snake-charmers are bad omens if met on the way. The noseless wife may either mean a dumb woman or a deformed one, another bad omen.

15. The god of love, Kāma, once tried to distract Śiva's penance. Śiva opened his fiery third eye and burned him down. From then on, Love became *anaṅga*, the bodiless or limbless one. Śiva's burning down of the god of Desire is the ideal paradigm for all ascetic conquest of temptations.

16. Local animal sacrifices, no less than Vedic sacrifices, are abhorrent to Vīraśaivas.

17. *Struck by an evil planet:* struck by misfortune, the action of malefic planets. The rich unregenerate worldling is a familiar target in the vacanas. cf. 820. The Vīraśaiva movement was a movement of the poor, the underdog.

18. *iron frame:* the original words *kabbunada kaṭṭu* are ambiguous. Here is an alternative translation:

    Look at them,
    busy, giving iron tonics
    to a bubble on the water
    to make it strong!

    It is customary in North Karnatak to give an 'iron decoction' – water boiled with iron – to weakling children to strengthen them.

19. Love of god, like liberty, is a matter of eternal vigilance. The traditional Indian metaphor for the 'strait and narrow path' is *asidhārāvrata*, 'walking the razor's edge'. Here the bhakta being sawn by the saw of bhakti is obverse of the traditional 'walking on the razor's edge'.

    The cobra in the pitcher is one of many ordeals or truth-tests to prove one's trustworthiness, chastity, etc. Other such tests are walking on fire, drinking poison.

20. The world as sea: cf. note on 8.

21. Liṅga and jaṅgama are one. Jaṅgama is Śiva's devotee, his representative on earth; literally jaṅgama means 'the moving man'. cf. 820.

22. 84 and its various multiples are familiar figures in Indian esoteric literature: 84 is the number of yogic postures; and the number of *Siddhas* (occult masters); the soul goes through a cycle of 84,000 births.

23. *I drink the water we wash your feet with:* a Vīraśaiva ritual, *pādodaka.* The devout Vīraśaiva washes the feet of his guru and imbibes the water as holy. Offerings of food, or *prasāda,* are also part of the guru-worship ritual (cf. Introduction, p. 33). Note also how the lord is not satisfied with even Vīraśaiva ritual offerings. Nindāstuti, the ambivalent, invective-like invocation or prayer to a god, is a well-known genre of Indian religious poetry. Here, for instance, the god is called a whore.

24. The familiar vacana opposition of *measure v. spontaneity.* Iamb and dactyl are here used as loose English equivalents for the Kannaḍa *amrtagaṇa* and *dēvagana,* kinds of metrical unit.

25. This and the next three poems attack idolatry: the folk-worship of menial gods, man-made images, vessels, trees and rivers.

26. One of the earliest references to the 'lost wax method' of making images.

27. The allusion is to the sacrificial fire of Vedic ritual. Vīraśaivism has no fire-rituals.

28. The bisexuality of the bhakta – cf. Mahādēvi 68, Dāsimayya 133.

29. cf. Introduction, pp. 19–22.

30. *cupola: kalaśa,* often translated 'pinnacle'.

31. *things standing:* sthāvara, the static temple.

32. *things moving:* jaṅgama, the living moving representative of Liṅga on the earth.

33. The master/servant stance (*dāsa-bhāva*).

DĀSIMAYYA

34. The phrase *karagadantiriside* in the first sentence is ambiguous and can also be rendered thus:

You balanced the globe
on the waters
like a pot on a dancer's head.

35. The punctuation in the Haḷakaṭṭi edition is obviously wrong. I have made a small correction in the punctuation to make sense of the syntax.
36. As in 35, I have corrected the punctuation to make sense of the syntax. The first lines suggest that large assemblies do not act, only the king gets to give charities – just as only one in a thousand gets to kill the enemy and the rest die routine deaths.
37. *Rider of the Bull:* a mythological attribute of Śiva. Such attributes are rarely mentioned in these poems. However, the phrase *nandívāhana* may also refer to Śiva's 'bull-riding minions,' his *gaṇas.*
38. The contrast in this vacana between the *bhakta* 'devotee, man of the lord', and the *bhavi* 'worldly man' is a favourite contrast with the vacana-poets. As in this vacana, *bhavi* usually means also a non-Vīraśaiva; the contrast is not without its overtones of zealotry as Christian/heathen, Jew/Gentile.
39. The *eighteen links* are the traditional eighteen bonds listed in Hindu texts: past, present, and future acts; body, mind, and wealth, substance, life, and self-regard; gold, land, and woman; lust, anger, greed, infatuation, pride, and envy.
40. *and bathes in a million sacred rivers:* this could also be, 'or bathes in Kōṭitīrtha,' a sacred place on the Narmada river.

MAHĀDĒVIYAKKA

41. I have, as elsewhere, taken the liberty of translating literally into English the name of Śiva here, Cennamallikārjuna. For such names carry aspects and attributes of Śiva. Further, such proper nouns, if left as they are in the English translation, are inert and cannot participate in the poems as they do in the originals. Other possible translations of the name are 'Arjuna of Jasmines' or 'Arjuna, Lord of goddess Mallika'. 'Arjuna' means 'white, bright'.

    The first four similes for the mystery of immanence are traditional, and used by other vacana writers as well.

42. A fresh use of conventional metaphor, 'milk and water'. When milk and water are mingled, no-one can separate them, except the legendary swan gifted in discrimination. The swan is the wisdom of the guru.
43. Akka has several complex attitudes towards the body – rejection, indifference and qualified acceptance. cf. also 17, 104, 117, 157. Her attitude to clothes and modesty are also part of her 'body-image'.
44. The spider and its web-house of illusions is an ancient Indian image for Māyā or Illusion. Here Akka appropriately changes the spider into a silkworm. (cf. Introduction, p. 41).
45. *eighty-four hundred thousand:* cf. note on Basavaṇṇa 430. Karma and the chain of births are cut short by bhakti. Bhakti, and its faith in the Lord's grace, is the answer to the inexorable logic of Karma.
46. Akka, more than all other vacanakāras, is aware of the world of nature. Hers is an outdoor world. cf. 73, 74, etc.
47. One of the few descriptions in vacanas of Śiva as a personal god, with a crown of diamonds. 'All men are His wives' gives another turn to Akka's attitude to human males – transforming her love of the lord as representative of all human/divine relations. Śiva and Śakti, the Lord and his Creative Power, are the eternal primordial pair in tantra and in yoga.
48. *mother: avva* could be her own mother, or any female companion.
49. The *koil* is the Indian cuckoo.
50. *parts of the day: jāva* or Sanskrit *yāma*, a unit equal to about three hours.
51. Śiva (unlike the crowned image of 68) is here seen in his more normal aspect, as an ascetic – a captivating, not forbidding ascetic.
52. *avva*, as in 69, a general vocative for female addressees. Unlike other poems (e.g. 69), this poem is apparently addressed to her own mother.
53. Here two words are used, *avva* and *avve*, the latter meaning her own mother. This is emphasized by the last part of the poem.
54. This vacana is part of Akka's answer to Allama according to *Śūnyasaṁpādane* (cf. p. 112). Allama asked why Akka is using her hair to cover her body while she professed to have given up all.

She replied that the skin will fall off when the fruit is really ripe. He counters it with 'You don't know whether you're in the lord or the lord in you. If the skin breaks before its time, the juice within will rot.' To this she answered with vacana 104 – till one has full knowledge of good and evil (*guṅadōṣa*), the body is still the house of passions etc.; nor can you reach the lord without such knowing. She is going through such an ordeal by knowledge. cf. 251, which continues her reply.

55. *round nut: beḷavalada kāyi*, a large unripe hard-shelled nut.

56. The interiorization of ritual offering. (cf. Introduction). Compare it with 131, where ritual is rendered unnecessary because all nature is in a state of worship.

57. Reference to her nakedness, her defiance of notions of modesty.

58. Leaf and flower as well as lamps and camphorfire are regular offerings (*pūje*) to the lord in homes and temples. Here, Akka sees day and night offering such worship themselves, replacing ritual.

59. This poem on the body is usually cited as Akka's answer to Allama's challenge: 'As long as you carry the pollutions of a body and the [five] senses, you cannot even touch the Lord.'

60. In the way of bhakti, it is customary to reject privilege and comfort, and court exile and beggary – in an effort to denude oneself and to throw oneself entirely on the lord's mercy.

61. 274 is supposedly Akka's exclamation on reaching the paradisal Sriśaila, the Holy Mountain. The All-giving Tree, the life-reviving herb etc. are all attributes of an alchemist's paradise, a paradise that various occult sects seek, where there is no want, disease, base metal, or unfulfilled wish. The plantain grove was the abode of Gorakhnātha, the master-magician or Siddha – cf. note on Allama.

62. Addressed to men who molested her, when she wandered naked.

63. The hero's going to war is one of the conventional reasons for separation of lovers in Indian love-poetry.

64. The typical accompaniments of fulfilled love, like soft breeze and moonlight, do not comfort a love-sick woman; they burn. Another conventional reason for separation is the lover's pique.

65. *lovebird: jakkavakki* or *cakravāka*, a fabled bird that cannot live apart from its mate.

ALLAMA PRABHU

The word prabhu, 'lord, master', is an honorific title added to the name Allama. There are controversies about the name Allama as well as his signature-line Guhēśvara, here translated as 'lord of caves'. Guhēśvara is one of Śiva's names and points up His yogic aspects. It is significant that Allama, preoccupied with awareness and ignorance, obsessed with images of light and darkness, should have chosen Guhēśvara as his favourite name for Śiva. Several forms of the name appear in the texts: Guhēśvara, Gohēśvara, Gogēśvara, Goggēśvara.

66. *Five men:* the five senses.
67. Koilbirds (Indian cuckoos, songbirds) come to mango trees in springtime. Both are celebrated in Indian poetry as indispensable to spring.
68. Mountain gooseberry and salt from the sea, though far from each other in origin, come together in the preparation of gooseberry pickle. Allama here alludes to a common Kannada proverb, as in the first sentence he alludes to a common poetic theme.
69. A beḍagina vacana, a 'fancy poem' or riddle poem (see Introduction p. 48). L. Basavarāju's edition contains several traditional commentaries on the esoteric symbolism of such poems. The following notes are directly indebted to L. Basavarāju's collations.

    Poem 95 may be glossed as follows: ignorance (the bee) born in the heart, obscures the light, overturns the worlds, even though it begins in a small way. Only when one realizes the impermanence of the body (five-coloured cage of the swan, traditional symbol for the soul), does the bee lose its power.
70. Another riddle poem. The liṅga (or Śiva) is born in the heart, manifests itself in the hand as an *iṣṭaliṅga* for action and worship. (For the different liṅgas, see Appendix I.) The camphor is self-awareness, perhaps because camphor sublimates, burns without residue. The pearl (by a pun on the word *mukti*, meaning both pearl and salvation) is a symbol of salvation. Diamonds are the

cosmic meanings. The blue sapphire is Māye, illusion. Note the dazzling use of synaesthesia, the surrealist 'disarrangement of the senses', to express mystical experience.

71. In this superb and difficult vacana, Allama speaks about the different stages of ignorance and realization. The triple city represents the three kinds of bodies everyone has: *sthūla* or the gross (material, perishable), *sūkṣma* or the subtle (invested by the material frame), liṅga or the imperishable original of the gross visible body. The triple city has one main gate, life-in-the-world or *saṁsāra*. The mind-monkey mocks every comer, even the king (soul) with his army (senses). The mind-monkey has form and movement, but no awareness (no head); one can see it move, but not track down its movements (legs without foot-steps); it has a will but no grasp (hand without fingers). Self-love (the wild elephant) is his offspring, which he rides and plays tricks on. Capturing the tenfold senses (ten-hooded snake) held in his will (basket), he blindfolds the five higher Powers (five virgins = the five *śaktis: icchā* or wish, *kriyā* or power of action, *mantra* or power of the word, *ādi* or the primal creativity, *parā* or the transcendent power; see Appendix I) with *saṁsāra* or worldliness. The lion in the ten streets is the life-breath in the ten paths of the body; the monkey tramples on the life-breath – but in this contact with the breath of life, he reaches enlightenment, holding true knowledge (diamond) in his will (hand). The last section describes the experience of such enlightenment: 'nothing added, nothing taken'. (For the Liṅga of the Breath or *prāṇaliṅga*, see Appendix I.)

72. For explanation, see Introduction, p. 48.

73. A description of enlightenment. The sky is the soul, the toad is the life-breath in its highest centre (*brahmarandra*); Rāhu the cosmic serpent (see note on Basavaṇṇa 9) is the serpent-path that winds through the body's centres (*cakras*) awakened by yoga. (For the *cakras*, see M. Eliade's *Yoga*, pp. 241–5.) Nowhere are the complex relationships between bhakti, tantra and yoga more richly expressed than in these vacanas of Allama. He uses yogic and tantric imagery and terminology, alludes to their techniques of ecstasy, yet finally rejects them in favour of bhakti,

grace, awareness. See pp. 145–7. The blind man is the devotee who sees without the benefit of eyes and grasps the cosmic serpent.

74. The cat is supreme knowledge, the rooster worldly knowledge. When supreme knowledge takes over worldly concern, the latter 'dies into life'. The black koilbird is the power of action or *kriyāśakti*, who takes over revealed knowledge (sun). The mind (casket) is abolished, only the experience (sacred thread) remains. No one can trace the process of enlightenment (footstep on the water); the experience of God (the sound of the word Guhēśwara) is indivisible, cannot be located as being here or there.

75. In the soul (sky) grows the wilderness (unawareness). Desire (the hunter) hunts down life (deer). Till life ends, desire has no end either.

76. The smell is *vāsanā*, 'latencies', the smell of past lives. As often in these riddle poems, the symbol is suggested by a pun: *vāsanā*, while a technical term for 'latencies', literally means 'smell'. Poetic, mystical as well as dream-symbols are often such puns.

The bee here is perfect knowledge of god (note the different meaning for bee in Allama 95). Heart (*manas*) and mind as intellect (*buddhi*) are distinguished here. The temple is the body (see Basavaṇṇa 820).

77. The city-limits symbolize the physical limits of the body; the temple, the inner mental form (*citpiṇḍa*). The power of knowledge, or *jñānaśakti*, is the hermit-woman, holding the mind (needle) on which are balanced the fourteen worlds. When the great enlightenment begins (the ant), it devours all these distinctions.

78. This vacana speaks of the devotee's discipline: the conquest of the eye's illusions, the burning-away of the heart's self-will and self-doubt, the intervening creations of language.

79. Awareness (tree) arises after the clearing of the physical nature (land without soil), yields eight kinds of subtle bodies (flowers) that become fruit on the branches (of right living), finally reaching basic (root) knowledge.

80. In the natural body (city), made of the five elements, arises the fire of supreme knowledge which burns the forest of worldly life – after which this very fire returns to consume the body.

81. The body is made of the five elements. Four are mentioned here: water, fire, wind, sky. The policeman is the devotee's awareness; the king and his two ministers are apparently the soul, its will and its history (or conduct). The nine-gated city is the body with its nine openings. The 9,000 men are the impressions of the many inner and outer senses.

82. Past, future, and present are conquered by the devotee. To such a devotee, even Viṣṇu and Brahma (two out of the great Hindu trinity, Viṣṇu, Brahma and Śiva) are sidekicks. The mind-*śakti* (*cicchakti*, Appendix I) is born (daughter) of Śiva-consciousness, the devotee is wedded to it – hence he is the son-in-law of Śiva. 500 is an excellent example of some vacana-characteristics: the familiar irreverence towards the great gods, the cheeky name-dropping, the playful use of deeper meanings and esoteric categories.

83. The poem alludes to praḷayas or 'deluges' that end each of the four eras of the cycle of creation.

84. References to symbolic conceptions of immanence: fire is hidden in wood and grass (which makes them inflammable; seeds of self in stone-like insensitiveness. The reflections of water are the illusions of a mind never still; the smell of wind is the smell of past lives, the latencies (see note on 429), that attend the breath of life. The body's heat (fire) has in it the sap of worldly desire. The carnal tongue must learn to taste the sunshine of awareness, must 'taste the light'.

85. *mortar without water:* the body purged of mind's will and its distortions.

pestle without shadows: the sense of the One.

women without bodies: the six Powers or *śaktis* (see Appendix I).

rice without grains: truth being pounded and purified.

the barren woman's son: the Unborn Lord, without beginnning or end.

86. This vacana describes the last stages of the process of enlightenment. The wind is the devotee's life-breath; the sky, the soul; the lullabies are the words *śivōham śivōham*, 'I am Śiva, I am Śiva.'

87. The waterfire refers to the belief that the oceans contain a core of fire.